The Financial Reporting Project and Readings

2nd Edition

For Learning Teams or Individuals

Bruce A. Baldwin
Arizona State University - West

SOUTH-WESTERN College Publishing
An International Thomson Publishing Company

Accounting Team Director: Richard K. Lindgren
Senior Acquisitions Editor: David L. Shaut
Developmental Editor: Sara E. Wilson
Production Editor: Rebecca A. Glaab
Marketing Manager: Matthew Filimonov
Manufacturing Coordinator: Gordon Woodside

ISBN: 0-538-87940-8

1 2 3 4 5 6 7 MZ 4 3 2 1 0 9 8

Printed in the United States of America

I(T)P®
International Thomson Publishing
South-Western College Publishing is an ITP Company. The ITP trademark is used under license.

HOW TO DOWNLOAD FINANCIAL REPORTS FROM THE Security and Exchange Commission's WEB SITE (the EDGAR database)

1. Sign on the Internet and go to the following address: **www.sec.gov/edaux/formlynx.htm**
2. In the "Select the form" box, select **10-K**.
3. In the "Enter a company" box, type the name of the company you want. For example, you might type in **General Mills**.
4. In the "What data range?" box, select **Entire database**.
5. Click on the "Submit Choices" button.
6. When the next screen appears, you will probably see a list of documents. Select the latest 10-K report by placing the cursor on the company name next to the latest date and clicking on the name.
7. Wait for the document to load. Some documents are long and require several minutes.
8. Save the file to disk. DO NOT PRINT. Some documents are over a hundred pages long.
9. Sign off the Internet.
10. Open the saved document in WORD (or another word processor; all references here are to WORD). The file is saved as a text file (.txt). Set the option of "Files of type" in the File, Open menu to **All Files** to see the .txt files you have saved.
11. Select the entire document (in the Edit menu, click on **Select All**.) Set the font to **Courier New** and the font size to **8**. In the File, Page Setup menu, set right and left margins to **0.5"**. This adjustment usually will ensure each line will be readable. Do not reformat the document. If you do, you probably will not be able to read the financial statements without a lot of realigning of text.
12. Find the financial statements in the document. They usually appear near the end of the document. You can use the Edit, Find menu to search for key words such as "financial statements, income statement, statement of earnings, etc." You must use trial and error because companies use various terms for their statements.
13. Highlight the financial statements and accompanying notes that follow the statements, and print these pages (click on **Selection** under Page range in File, Print menu) or cut and paste them into a new document for later access.
14. Save the original 10-K document as a WORD file for future reference.

PREFACE to the 2nd Edition

TO STUDENTS: The primary purpose of **The Financial Reporting Project** is for you to experience up-to-date "live" financial statements "in their natural habitat." For most users of financial statements, the natural habitat is the Annual Report to Stockholders or the SEC Form 10-K Report. While portions of real financial statements are illustrated in your textbook, this project will "put it all together." You will work with the complete and integrated financial reports of a real company as you apply the lessons of your accounting course. The development and application of this accounting knowledge will advance your career.

Be aware that, occasionally, some of the ratio formulas you use in this project are slightly different from the ratio formulas that may be used in your textbook. This is because, in practice, different credit managers or financial analysts use a variety of different formulas. For many ratios there is no standard formula. In this project, I tend to use the formulas used by Dun & Bradstreet or RMA Associates, two of the premier companies that gather and report this type of information. Sometimes the "real-world" formulas are just a bit more complex that those used in textbooks, sometimes they are simpler. Often, the slightly different formulations do not have a material effect on the result.

A secondary purpose of **The Financial Reporting Project** is to familiarize you with common sources of business and financial information. Employers expect that you are able to quickly and accurately obtain business and financial information about suppliers, customers, or competitors. Many of the assignments in this project will require you to use classic reference sources from the library (or the Internet) that are used everyday in the business world.

A third purpose of **The Financial Reporting Project** is to build teamwork skills. Many employers have made the following remark to me. "You professors educate students one-at-a-time but we employers work them in teams." Today, employers expect that you will have experience working closely on team-oriented projects. You may already know that teamwork skills take time and effort to develop. This is all part of your education and failure to develop and extend your teamwork skills is just as dangerous to your career as failing to master personal computer, writing, and speaking skills.

TO PROFESSORS: In this edition, I have integrated Internet web sites into the assignments. Where appropriate, students are guided to the Baldwin homepage at **http://www.baldwin.swcollege.com**. After selecting **The Financial Reporting Project,** students select the current assignment they are working on and obtain hot links to free web sites relevant to the assignment. All assignments, however, can still be completed using only traditional library resources.

This project is the result of many years of experimentation with students in my own classes. I've always been concerned that my students be able to successfully make the transition from classroom topics and textbook examples to the use and understanding of "real" financial statements. **The Financial Reporting Project** (which includes analysis the Annual Report, the SEC 10-K and the Proxy Statement) is designed to achieve this. An unanticipated side benefit of this project has been that students like dealing with "live" financial information. I've often been amazed at how students will pore over the annual reports, proxy statements and SEC 10-Ks that they have received in the mail or downloaded from the Internet. When they run into complicated issues their curiosity is piqued, and they want to know more. Students are also intrigued by current readings. Each reading expands on an issue or topic related to the corresponding assignment. I've used **The Financial Reporting Project** successfully in the sophomore-level introductory accounting course and in the MBA financial accounting course.

Learning Groups: While this project is a valuable tool when completed by students working individually, I believe its learning benefits are maximized when it is completed by student-teams. My strategy has been to assign a different company to each group in the class. Each student obtains his/her own copy of the annual report, the 10-K, and the proxy statement. The assigned company can then be used for a variety of in-class and out-of-class team-based assignments. Each team-member is expected to become an expert regarding his/her company and then contribute that knowledge to an end-of-semester written report prepared by the group. Often I have teams make end-of-semester class presentations based on their written report. If you assign students to work individually, use Assignments 1-A and 4-A. If your students will work in groups, use Assignments 1-B and 4-B, instead. All other assignments can be used by either individuals or groups.

In the Instructor's Manual, I provide an alphabetized master-list of approximately 1,100 companies to make it easy to assign companies to students or student teams. In a second listing of these same firms, they are grouped by industry if you wish to focus on a specific industry or minimize such overlap. Each company is identified by name, primary stock exchange, and ticker symbol. The Instructor's Manual also provides a variety of hints and suggestions regarding use of **The Financial Reporting Project** (e.g., suggested guidelines about forming teams).

I am indebted to many persons for their assistance in bringing this project to fruition. Students, for example, provided many helpful criticisms of early versions of many assignments. Faculty colleagues did the same. Special thanks to Sara Wilson of South-Western Publishing who provided much encouragement and many helpful suggestions during critical stages of development. All errors and omissions, however, are my personal responsibility. I hope you find this project helpful and useful. If you have suggestions for improvement, please call, write, or send email. I welcome your suggestions.

Bruce A. Baldwin
School of Management
Arizona State University West
P.O. Box 37100
Phoenix, Arizona 85069-7100

phone: (602)543-6210
fax: (602)543-6303
email: bruce_baldwin@fcgate.west.asu.edu

TABLE OF CONTENTS

Name: ______________________ Professor: ______________________

Course: ______________________ Section: ______________________

Assignment 1-A
CHOOSING A COMPANY
(for Individuals)

The purpose of *The Financial Reporting Project* is to apply the lessons of your accounting course to a real company. You will discover how the issues, topics, practices and procedures described in your textbook actually affect a company's financial reports. The first step is to choose a company that you think you will find interesting and that you want to know more about. Choose carefully because you will work with this company on several assignments this term. Be sure to choose a publicly-held U.S. company so that its financial information will be readily available. (Publicly-held means that its stock is traded on a stock exchange.) Your professor may give you additional guidelines on choosing a firm.

IDENTIFYING COMPANIES FROM WHICH TO CHOOSE:

Recognizing that your professor may have placed some limitations on your choice, here are some possible ways to go about identifying companies from which to choose.

1. You might first want to choose an industry that interests you. For example, a specific industry might be appealing because:

   a. Someone you know works in that industry or perhaps you have worked in a particular industry that you would like to learn more about.

   b. A company in that industry is located in your hometown or in a nearby location.

   c. You regularly purchase products from that industry (e.g., textbooks or beverages).

   d. The industry might be one that could provide employment opportunities after graduation.

   e. The industry has been in the news lately, and you are interested in being better informed about the issues that were raised.

2. A good place to start is in your school's library. Following are five sources that provide information about many industries and specific information about individual firms in those industries.

   a. *Forbes*, a bi-weekly business magazine published by Forbes, Inc. Its "Annual Report on American Industry" appears in the first January issue each year. It includes brief descriptions of 31 major industries and ranks industries and more than 1,000 leading companies by profits, growth, and stock market performance. Under each industry heading are listed the leading companies in that industry.

   b. *Value Line Investment Survey*, published by Value Line, Inc. This service is updated weekly and comes in three parts. The front page of Part 1 ("Summary & Index") lists about 100 industry categories along with the page number where information on each industry can be found in Part 3. In Part 3 you will find the industry information as well as specific information about each company in each industry.

   c. *Standard & Poor's Industry Surveys*, published by Standard & Poor's, Inc. This two-volume document is published every quarter and covers dozens of industries and hundreds of companies. In the front part of each volume you will find a section titled the "Earnings Supplement." This section lists all the industry categories and each of the companies within each industry.

   d. *Fortune*, a bi-weekly business magazine published by Time, Inc. Its annual listing of the 500 largest firms in the United States is referred to as the Fortune 500 and is probably the most widely cited listing of this type. The Fortune 500 usually is in the mid-April edition.

   e. *Standard Industrial Classification Manual*, published by the U.S. Government Office of Management & Budget. This manual organizes all businesses and industries in the United States into four-digit SIC codes. In the back of the volume is an alphabetical index of industry categories with the SIC code for each category. The front of the manual is a detailed description of each industry category. Use this manual to select an industry and its four-digit SIC code. After selecting an industry, go to the *Million Dollar Directory*, published by Dun & Bradstreet, Inc. The directory is a series of five volumes; look for the one labeled "Series Cross-Reference by Industry." This volume is organized by SIC code numbers. You will find many companies for whatever SIC code you have chosen along with each firm's mailing address and telephone number. (This information will be handy for Assignment 1-C.)

ON THE INTERNET: The Internet is a rich and growing source of financial information that can be used in this and other assignments. Convenient access is provided via the Baldwin homepage at **http://www.baldwin.swcollege.com.** To access Internet resources helpful for this assignment, go to the Baldwin homepage, select *The Financial Reporting Project* and explore the hot links listed under Assignment 1-A.

COMPLETING THE ASSIGNMENT:

1. What is the name of the company you have chosen?

____

2. Which industry category does your firm represent?

____

3. Write several paragraphs describing how (and why) you chose the firm you did. Did you use any of the resources listed earlier in this assignment, or the Internet? Were they easy to use? Hard to use? Which one(s) would you recommend to friends if they had to complete this assignment? Discuss.

   NOTE: Please think and plan carefully before writing. Readability, spelling, organization, grammar, and sentence structure will all be considered in grading your response.

____

____

____

____

____

____

____

____

____

____

____

Name: ______________________ Professor: ______________________

Course: ______________________ Section: ______________________

Assignment 1-B
ORGANIZING YOUR GROUP
(for Learning Teams)

The purpose of *The Financial Reporting Project* is to apply the lessons of your accounting course to real companies. You will discover how the issues, topics, practices and procedures described in your textbook actually affect companies' financial reports.

OVERVIEW OF THE GROUP PROJECT:

Your professor has already assigned your group a company (or companies) on which to focus. The final output of this project will be an analysis of the company (or companies) assigned to you.

If your group is required to evaluate several firms in the same industry, your first task will be to assign a specific company to each member of your group. This will be your first exercise in group decision making.

Each group member is expected to become very knowledgeable regarding one or all of your team's assigned companies. You will obtain the company's financial statements and other financial information (see Assignment 1 C) and observe how your firm implements the principles and practices that you will learn in this course. Later in the course you will begin to analyze and evaluate your individual firm's financial stability and trends. Also you will conduct library research to further familiarize yourself with your company and the industry in which your firm competes. If each team member has been assigned a different firm, the other members of your group will be doing the same thing for their firms (which compete with yours).

Each member will contribute his/her expertise regarding the assigned firm(s) to the group's report. Your group's project will be due on a date announced by your professor. There are more instructions on the group report and analysis in Assignment 15.

You should review those instructions very soon and begin (as a team) to develop strategies for completion of the project.

COMPLETING THE ASSIGNMENT:

1. In the space provided below, list the name, telephone number, and email address (if any) of each member of your team. This listing will help you keep in contact during the course.

	Group Member Names	Phone Numbers	Email Addresses
a.	____________________	__________	____________
b.	____________________	__________	____________
c.	____________________	__________	____________
d.	____________________	__________	____________
e.	____________________	__________	____________
f.	____________________	__________	____________

2. Choose a name for your group and write it in the space provided. Feel free to be creative. For example, you might want to select a name that is a clever play-on-words regarding the name of your company or industry. Your professor will probably appreciate the humor.

   Group name ______________________________

3. After completing this assignment (as a team) turn in one copy of the group information to your professor. Also, be sure that every team member has a complete set of the information in Part 1 above.

> **ON THE INTERNET:** The Internet is a rich and growing source of financial information that can be used in this and other assignments. Convenient access is provided via the Baldwin homepage at **http://www.baldwin.swcollege.com**. To access Internet resources helpful on various assignments in this book, go to the Baldwin homepage, select *The Financial Reporting Project* and explore the hot links listed there for the Assignment you are working on.

Name: ______________________________ Professor: ____________________

Course: ______________________________ Section: ____________________

Assignment 1-C
OBTAINING FINANCIAL STATEMENTS

Most future assignments will be based on information contained in your company's Annual Report, its SEC Form 10-K, and its proxy statement. In this assignment you are to contact your assigned (or chosen) company to request the most recent version of those items that is available.

The Annual Report is a document that must be distributed to all shareholders every year. It contains the firm's financial statements as well as a variety of other required and optional information. Often, it is a slick and glossy publication with color pictures of the executives, company facilities, and products. The SEC Form 10-K is the version of the annual report that must be filed annually with the Securities and Exchange Commission (an agency of the federal government in Washington, D.C.). When you receive your firm's Annual Report and SEC 10-K you will notice that the two documents have many similarities but that they also have some striking differences.

The proxy statement is a document describing matters that will be discussed or voted on at the annual stockholders' meeting. It is also the device by which management of the corporation solicits your authorization (proxy) to vote your shares on its behalf. Of greatest interest, perhaps, proxy statements must provide detailed information about compensation of key executive personnel. (Ever wonder how much money the top executives of a large corporation are paid? Here's your chance to find out.)

COMPLETING THE ASSIGNMENT:

1. Contact your company by telephone, letter, or email. You will need to go to your university library, community public library, or the Internet to obtain the mailing address, email address, or telephone number. The address, and usually the phone number, can be obtained from the following sources:

   a. *Directory of Corporate Affiliations*, National Register Publishing Co.

   b. *Million Dollar Directory*, Dun & Bradstreet

c. *Q-File*, Q-Data Corporation

d. *Reference Book of Corporate Management: America's Corporate Leaders*, Marketing Services, Inc.

> **ON THE INTERNET:** Web sites where you may be able to find this information for your company are listed on the Baldwin homepage. Go to **http://www.baldwin.swcollege.com**, select *The Financial Reporting Project*, and explore the hot links under Assignment 1-C.

2. The following hints will help you carry out this assignment.

   a. Companies usually have an Office of Investor Relations or Shareholder Relations. Write to, or telephone, that office. If your company has an Internet homepage, you may be able to send an email request directly.

   b. Explain that you are an accounting student at ______________________ (identify your school) and that as part of a class assignment this term you will be studying the firm and its financial information.

   c. Request a copy of the firm's most recent Annual Report, most recent SEC Form 10-K, and its most recent Proxy Statement. Be sure to tell them how much you appreciate their assistance. A little gratitude goes a long way in smoothing these requests. (Actually, most firms are very happy to provide these documents. They tend to think of you either as a potential investor, potential customer, or both. At minimum, it's usually great public relations for a firm to have college students interested in it.)

   d. Provide an **exact** mailing address. These documents are very important to you, and you do not want to risk having them mishandled because of a vague address.

3. Record the following information regarding your request.

   a. Post office address or email address of the firm (if you sent a letter or email):

      ____

      ____

      ____

   b. Date of request for documents: ______________________

c. Method of making the request (e.g., telephone, fax, letter, email):

____

d. Phone number of firm (if you telephoned or faxed): ______________

SAMPLE LETTER:

If you prefer to write a letter, it could be similar to the following:

(Your Name and Address)

(Today's Date)

Investor Relations Department
Humble Pie Bakery Corporation
3652 Modesty Boulevard
Ovenhot, Arizona 00000

Director of Investor Relations:

I am an accounting student at ______________ (name your school). As part of a class assignment this term all students will be examining and analyzing the financial reports of a major corporation.

I have chosen your firm and would like to study the financial reports of your company as part of my class assignment. Please assist me by sending me a copy of your most recent Annual Report, most recent SEC 10-K, and most recent Proxy Statement. Thank you very much for your help!

Sincerely,

(Type your name on this line and put your signature just above it.)

Name: ______________________ Professor: ______________________

Course: ______________________ Section: ______________________

Assignment 2
BASIC COMPANY INFORMATION

Name of your company: ______________________

The purpose of this assignment is to help you obtain background information about your firm. The first step toward understanding a firm's financial information is to understand the company itself.

COMPLETING THE ASSIGNMENT:

1. For each of the items below that you use in completing this assignment, be sure to indicate in the space provided the edition (or year of the edition) that you used. If some of the suggested references are not available in your library your reference librarian may be able to suggest other sources that you could use instead. Many resources that summarize basic company information are now available, perhaps in *your* library, on CD-ROM.

Reference	Edition Used
a. *The Corporate Directory of U.S. Public Companies*, Walker's Western Research	______
b. *Million Dollar Directory*, Dun & Bradstreet, Inc.	______
c. *Moody's Industrial Manual* (or Transportation, Public Utilities, or Bank & Finance manuals), Moody's Investor Service, Inc.	______
d. *Standard & Poors Register of Corporations, Directors, and Executives*, Standard & Poor's, Inc.	______
e. *Standard & Poor's Corporation Records*, S&P, Inc.	______
f. *Directory of Corporate Affiliations*, National Register Publishing Company	______
g. *America's Corporate Families*, Dun & Bradstreet, Inc.	______

ON THE INTERNET: Sometimes, different companies have similar names. To provide exact identification, web sites usually request you to type in the company's stock ticker symbol. (The stock ticker symbol is a one-to-five letter code under which the company's stock trades on the stock exchanges.) As soon as possible, identify your company's stock ticker symbol. It will make your search for information easier. You can find your firm's stock ticker symbol by going to the Baldwin homepage at **http://www.baldwin.swcollege.com**, select *The Financial Reporting Project*, and clicking on the Stock Ticker Symbol button listed under Assignment 2.

NOTE: Web sites appear or disappear suddenly. Sometimes data that *was* free suddenly requires a fee. I monitor the web and update the Baldwin homepage regularly to keep the list of free web sites as current as possible.

2. Use the library references listed on the prior page, or Internet sources, to obtain the information requested below and to answer the questions that follow. *(Please think and plan carefully before answering the questions. Readability, organization, spelling, grammar, and sentence structure will all be considered in grading your responses.)*

   a. Basic company facts:

      1. Complete name of firm: ______________________________

      2. State in which the company is incorporated: ____________________

      3. Year in which the company was founded: ______________________

      4. Primary and secondary SIC codes (see Reading 2): ______________

      5. Independent auditor: ______________________________

      6. Stock exchange(s) where its shares are traded: ________________

         ____

      7. Stock ticker symbol: ____________

b. Describe the products your company offers and type(s) of customers to whom those products are probably sold.

c. Is your company a large company? Identify several measures that could be used to describe the "size" of a company. How does your firm measure up on those attributes?

d. Describe the composition of your company's Board of Directors (e.g., age, gender, background experience, etc.)

e. Is your company part of a "group" of companies? For example, does it have subsidiaries? Is your firm a subsidiary of some other firm? Discuss.

3. What are the most interesting aspects of your company (or its industry) that you have discovered so far? Discuss.

Reading 2

A Note Regarding SIC Codes and NAICS Codes

Since the 1930s, the Standard Industrial Classification (SIC) Code has been a simple coding system used by the U.S. federal government to gather, classify and report information on U.S. businesses. The SIC system, which has been refined and updated every ten to fifteen years, has been widely adopted as a standard for defining and analyzing industry structure. During the 1990s revision, this business classification system was reworked in cooperation with Canada and Mexico so that comparable business statistics could be obtained for the three NAFTA trading partners. The SIC coding system was renamed the North American Industry Classification System (NAICS) and the first complete manual of classifications was published in Spring 1998. The first NAICS data is expected in 1999 and 2000. Until then, U.S. economic data continues to be reported using the SIC code system. This system divides virtually all economic activity into 10 major categories:

Agriculture, Forestry, and Fishing............ 01-09
Mining.. 10-14
Construction.. 15-17
Manufacturing.. 20-39
Transport, Communications, Utilities........ 40-49
Wholesale Trade....................................... 50-51
Retail Trade 52-59
Finance, Insurance, Real Estate............... 60-67
Services 70-89
Public Administration 90-97

Each line of business is classified into one of these 10 categories and assigned a four digit code. The first two digits are referred to as the Major Group Code that describes the general nature of the activity. For example:

Major Group 78 . . . MOTION PICTURES

The third and fourth digits of the SIC Code describe the specific activity:

7812 . . . Motion Picture and Video Tape Production
7819 . . . Services Allied to Motion Picture Production
7822 . . . Motion Picture and Video Tape Distribution

Under both the SIC system and the NAICS system, many companies can be categorized under several different "lines of business" and therefore, are assigned several codes. The line of business which represents the largest percentage of sales is known as the Primary Code, others are referred to as Secondary Codes.

Generally, when multiple codes are listed for a single firm, they are presented in descending order of their percentage of the firm's sales volume. The primary code is listed first (largest percentage of sales) and secondary codes are then listed in descending order of their respective sales percentages.

The NAICS approach, when fully implemented, will be more detailed that the SIC system it replaces. It uses 20 classifications rather than 10 and identifies industries by 6-digit codes. This allows greater detail in classifications and flexibility in identifying subsectors within industries. The NAICS agreement among the U.S., Canada, and Mexico fixes only the first five digits of the code. The sixth digit, if used, can be designated by the individual countries for their own economic reporting purposes.

Name: ______________________ Professor: ______________

Course: ______________________ Section: ______________

Assignment 3
THE ECONOMIC, SOCIAL, LEGAL AND POLITICAL ENVIRONMENT

Name of your company ______________________________

This assignment sends you to the library (and/or to the Internet) to do some background reading about your firm. Financial statements are best understood when the reader comprehends fully the economic, social, legal and political environment in which the firm operates. The purpose of this assignment is for you to gain an understanding of that current environment. There may be important new legislation that has affected your firm, or perhaps there has been a recent management shakeup. New technology, new competitors, new social trends, or legal battles could all affect the general financial health of your firm.

KEY REFERENCES FOR THIS ASSIGNMENT:

Following is a sampling of bibliographic indexes that college and university libraries typically have available. Remember, this is just a sample. Not all libraries will have all of the these items and most libraries will have others. The following list is provided to help you get started. A major purpose of this assignment is to develop your skills in library (and/or Internet) research by gaining familiarity with typical sources of business information. Space has been provided for you to write in any additional sources you find and use.

References	Available in your library?	Did you use it?
a. *ABI-Inform*, UMI, Inc (on CD-ROM)	______	______
b. *Accountants Index*, American Institute of Certified Public Accountants	______	______
c. *Business Newsbank*, Newsbank, Inc. (on CD-ROM)	______	______
d. *Business Periodicals Index*, H.W. Wilson Company	______	______

e. *Predicast F&S Index*, Predicasts _______ _______

f. *The New York Times Index*, New York Times Co. _______ _______

g. *The Wall Street Journal Index*, Dow Jones & Co. _______ _______

Other References Used

h. ____

i. ____

> **ON THE INTERNET:** Alternatively, or in addition to your library search, you may want to "surf the net" for background information about your firm. Go to the Baldwin homepage at **http://www.baldwin.swcollege.com**, select *The Financial Reporting Project*, and explore the hot links listed under Assignment 3.

COMPLETING THE ASSIGNMENT:

1. Use the sources suggested above to identify recent articles about your firm. Generally you should focus on articles that are no more than two years old. Select two recent articles concerning your company (no more than one article from a single source listed above). Find the article, read it, and if you believe it conveys significant and interesting information, photocopy it (or download it) to turn in with this assignment. Note: It is a serious breach of academic integrity to tear articles out of magazines that do not belong to you...e.g., those in the library. Please don't do it!

2. Index (website) used to find article #1 ________________________________

3. Citation for article #1:

   i. Name of periodical ____

   ii. Title of article____

   iii. Date of periodical ________________

   iv. Page numbers __________

4. Article analysis: Describe why this article is significant and interesting. Limit your response to no more than 100 carefully chosen words. Use complete sentences.

____

____

____

____

____

____

____

____

____

____

____

____

____

5. Index (website) used to find article #2______________________________

6. Citation for article #2:

   i. Name of periodical ______________________________

   ii. Title of article ______________________________

   iii. Date of periodical ______________

   iv. Page numbers __________

7. Article analysis: In the space provided below and on the next page, describe why this article is significant and interesting. Limit your response to no more than 100 carefully chosen words. Use complete sentences.

____

____

____

8. Attach photocopies of the articles to this assignment.

Reading 3

Universal Accounting Rules Prove Elusive

Slow Pace Delays Jump in Foreign Listings in U.S.

By ELIZABETH MACDONALD
Staff Reporter of The Wall Street Journal

The struggle for a universal set of accounting standards is proving to be tougher than expected, frustrating hopes for a sharp expansion of foreign listings on U.S. stock exchanges.

A report issued by the Financial Accounting Standards Board this week could further dash hopes by spelling out just how much more work needs to be done. Many foreign companies want to list on U.S. exchanges, but only if they can report financial results and other information using foreign accounting standards rather than the more rigid U.S. rules. At the same time, many U.S. investors and regulators fear reliance on foreign standards. The solution to the conflict depends on resolving differences between foreign and U.S. rules.

For the past nine years, the International Accounting Standards Committee (IASC), which makes international accounting rules, and the International Organization of Securities Commissions have been slogging away at a core set of international accounting standards that foreign companies could use to directly list on U.S. exchanges and other global markets. Once the rules are completed, the U.S. Securities and Exchange Commission is expected to consider letting foreign companies use them in U.S. markets.

Confident of Progress

Last April, the London-based IASC felt so confident of its progress that it said its rules would be ready in March 1998, a year earlier than expected. "We want governments around the world to let foreign companies use our standards, so they can be accepted in any market in the world," said Liesel Knorr, technical director of the IASC.

But the FASB report shows that the international rule makers "have a long way to go," said Dennis R. Beresford, chairman of the group, the main rule-making body for American accountants. The study spotlighted 255 discrepancies between IASC rules and U.S. generally accepted accounting principles.

"I think the study shows that it's proving to be difficult for the IASC to close these significant gaps," said Jeannot Blanchet, the Arthur Andersen partner in charge of European IASC issues in Paris. "The bar has been elevated in terms of what the IASC has to do to meet SEC demands for high quality accounting standards."

The FASB study says that the IASC has yet to draw up accounting rules that explicitly address such issues as post-retirement benefits, stock-based compensation, mortgage servicing rights and troubled debt restructuring. The international rule makers have also generally ignored accounting rules for futures contracts and hedging, loan impairment losses, financial instruments including derivatives, and loan fees, the report adds. Furthermore, the FASB says, the entire oil and gas industry has yet to flicker across the IASC's accounting screen.

Aiming for 1998 Goal

The IASC's Ms. Knorr said, "That's all true, but hopefully by March 1998 we will have rules on most of these issues."

But FASB officials see problems ahead. "There are some basic, glaring differences," said Mr. Beresford. "If these holes aren't plugged, it will be difficult, and in some cases impossible, for U.S. investors to properly compare a foreign company's net income with that of U.S. firms."

Currently, foreign companies selling securities in the U.S. must report financial results based on U.S. accounting standards. They may use their own home-country standards only if they also report results reconciled with U.S. rules. Since 1989, the IASC has been battling with FASB to let it be the international standard setter for foreign companies.

"The temptation to water down accounting standards to get big foreign companies to list in the U.S.'s deep, wide and liquid markets has never been greater," said Prof. Louis Lowenstein, professor emeritus of finance and law at Columbia University. The New York Stock Exchange, with its $7.4 trillion capitalization, is hungry for foreign listings, both to increase its own profits and to maintain its spot at the top of world markets.

Big Board's Role

The Big Board has been working behind the scenes to get the FASB and the SEC to allow more big foreign companies to list here, a Big Board spokesman notes. Foreign companies, too, seek listings in global markets to raise cross-border capital. Even with the tough U.S. accounting rules, the number of foreign companies listing on the Big Board has nearly tripled in the last five years to 285 today. Since 1990, the number of foreign companies registering with the SEC has risen to 856 from 434.

The SEC is adamant that IASC strengthen its accounting standards. But the commission has already accommodated the IASC by letting foreign companies use certain IASC standards when they are sufficiently close to U.S. standards. For example, foreign companies can use IASC rules to account for hyperinflation, business combinations for cross-border stock filings, and cash-flow.

In recent years, the SEC has also exempted foreign companies from U.S. proxy and insider reporting rules. In addition, the commission lets foreign firms disclose executive compensation in the aggregate, rather than individually. "The SEC is holding out a carrot to the IASC to get it to keep improving its standards," Mr. Beresford said.

So far, the IASC is sticking to its March 1998 deadline.

The Wall Street Journal
December 6, 1996
Page A11A

QUESTIONS FOR CONSIDERATION:

1. Why would a foreign firm object to providing financial statements based on U.S. GAAP in return for allowing the firm's stock to be traded on U.S. exchanges?

2. Does it really matter which accounting standards are used by foreign companies wishing to list their stocks on U.S. exchanges? If so, to whom would it matter? Why?

Name: ______________________ Professor: ______________________

Course: ______________________ Section: ______________________

Assignment 4-A
INDUSTRY INFORMATION
(for Individuals)

Name of your company: ______________________

Industry category: ______________________

In prior assignments you have obtained a great deal of information about your chosen firm. By now you should have a good understanding of its background, its strengths, weaknesses, and current developments. This assignment shifts the focus from your specific firm to the industry of which your firm is a part. Overall trends within an industry generally have a large impact on the success of specific firms within the industry. As part of your prior reading you probably have obtained some insight into the nature of the industry in which your firm competes. This assignment is designed to further that understanding.

KEY REFERENCES FOR THIS ASSIGNMENT:

The following is a sampling of resources that college and university libraries typically have available. Remember, this is just a sample. Not all libraries will have all of these items and most libraries will have others. The following list is provided to help you get started. If you need assistance, ask the Reference Librarian. He/she will be glad to help. A major purpose of this assignment is to further develop your library (and/or Internet) research skills by gaining familiarity with additional classic sources of business information.

Following are four excellent sources of background information on industries.

Category 1 Sources:

a. *Standard & Poor's Industry Surveys*, published by Standard & Poor's, Inc. This two-volume reference is updated and published quarterly. It yields current industry information on 21 major industry groups that it further subdivides into 150 industry sub-groups. Also included is information on more than 1,000 companies that it classifies into the 150 subgroups.

b. *Value Line Investment Survey*, published by Value Line, Inc. This weekly service is comprised of three sections. The "Summary and Index" (Part 1) lists the page numbers in Part 3 where information regarding your industry category can be found. The *Value Line Investment Survey* tracks about 100 industry categories composed of more than 1700 specific companies.

c. *U.S. Industrial Outlook*, published annually by the U.S. Department of Commerce, contains industry reviews, analyses and forecasts for 350 industries. It also provides a profile of international competitiveness for each industry.

d. *Predicast Forecasts*, published by Predicasts, Inc. This volume organizes its industry forecasts by SIC Code and provides estimates of industry sales and annual growth rates.

These additional sources below can be used to identify news articles that have an industry focus.

Category 2 Sources:

a. *ABI-Inform*, UMI, Inc. (on CD-ROM)

b. *Accountants Index*, American Institute of Certified Public Accountants

c. *Business Newsbank*, Newsbank, Inc. (on CD-ROM)

d. *Business Periodicals Index*, H.W. Wilson Company

e. *The New York Times Index*, New York Times Company

f. *The Wall Street Journal Index*, Dow-Jones & Company

g. Almost every industry has an industry periodical (such as *Progressive Grocer* in the supermarket business or *Advertising Age* in the advertising business). This would be a good source of information about issues facing the industry.

ON THE INTERNET: Alternatively, or in addition to your library search, you may want to "surf the net" for trends and developments affecting your company's industry. Go to the Baldwin homepage at **http://www.baldwin.swcollege.com,** select *The Financial Reporting Project*, and explore the hot links listed under Assignment 4.

COMPLETING THE ASSIGNMENT:

1. Use one or more sources from Category 1 to familiarize yourself with trends and developments within your chosen industry. (Do **not** use the Internet as a source of information for this portion of the assignment.)

a. Which Category 1 source(s) did you consult? ______________________________

____

____

b. What major trends and developments are occurring in your industry? Summarize the information you obtained from Category 1 sources. Answer this question essay-style using complete sentences.

____

____

____

____

____

____

____

____

____

____

____

____

____

____

____

____

____

____

2. Use one or more of the Category 2 sources suggested above (or the Internet) to identify recent articles about your industry. Generally you should focus on articles that are no more than two years old. Select two recent articles concerning your industry (no more than one article from a single index). Find each article, read it, and if you believe it conveys significant and interesting information, photocopy it to turn in with this assignment. If not, keep looking until you find such an article.

   a. Index used to find article#1: ______________________________

   b. Citation for article #1:

      i. Name of periodical ______________________________

      ii. Title of article ______________________________

      iii. Date of periodical ______________

      iv. Page numbers __________

   c. Article analysis: Describe why the information in article #1 is important to your industry? Limit your response to no more than 100 words and use complete sentences.

____

____

____

____

____

____

____

____

____

____

____

____

____

d. Index used to find article #2____________________________

e. Citation for article #2:

i. Name of periodical ____________________________

ii. Title of article ____________________________

iii. Date of periodical ______________

iv. Page numbers __________

f. Article analysis: Why is article #2 interesting and significant to your firm's industry? Limit your response to no more than 100 words and use complete sentences.

____

____

____

____

____

____

____

____

____

____

____

____

____

____

____

3. Attach photocopies of the articles to this assignment. (Note: It is a serious breach of academic integrity to tear articles out of magazines that do not belong to you...e.g., those in the library. Please don't do it!)

Name: ______________________ Professor: ______________________

Course: ______________________ Section: ______________________

Assignment 4-B
INDUSTRY INFORMATION
(for Learning Teams)

Name of your company: ______________________

Industry category: ______________________

In prior assignments you have obtained a great deal of information about your assigned firm. By now you should have a good understanding of its background, its strengths, weaknesses, and current developments. This assignment shifts the focus from your specific firm to the industry of which your firm is a part. Overall trends within an industry generally have a large impact on the success of specific firms within the industry. As part of your prior reading you probably have obtained some insight into the nature of the industry in which your firm competes. This assignment is designed to further that understanding.

KEY REFERENCES FOR THIS ASSIGNMENT:

The following is a sampling of resources that college and university libraries typically have available. Remember, this is just a sample. Not all libraries will have all of these items and most libraries will have others. The following list is provided to help you get started. If you need assistance, ask the Reference Librarian. He/she will be glad to help. A major purpose of this assignment is to further develop your library (and/or Internet) research skills by gaining familiarity with additional classic sources of business information.

Following are four excellent sources of background information on industries.

Category 1 Sources:

a. *Standard & Poor's Industry Surveys*, published by Standard & Poor's, Inc. This two-volume reference is updated and published quarterly. It yields current industry information on 21 major industry groups that it further subdivides into 150 industry sub-groups. Also included is information on more than 1,000 companies that it classifies into the 150 subgroups.

b. *Value Line Investment Survey*, published by Value Line, Inc. This weekly service is comprised of three sections. The "Summary and Index" (Part 1) lists the page numbers in Part 3 where information regarding your industry category can be found. The *Value Line Investment Survey* tracks about 100 industry categories composed of more than 1700 specific companies.

c. *U.S. Industrial Outlook*, published annually by the U.S. Department of Commerce, contains industry reviews, analyses and forecasts for 350 industries. It also provides a profile of international competitiveness for each industry.

d. *Predicast Forecasts*, published by Predicasts, Inc. This volume organizes its industry forecasts by SIC Code and provides estimates of industry sales and annual growth rates.

These additional sources below can be used to identify news articles that have an industry focus.

Category 2 Sources:

a. *ABI-Inform*, UMI, Inc. (on CD-ROM)

b. *Accountants Index*, American Institute of Certified Public Accountants

c. *Business Newsbank*, Newsbank, Inc. (on CD-ROM)

d. *Business Periodicals Index*, H.W. Wilson Company

e. *The New York Times Index*, New York Times Company

f. *The Wall Street Journal Index*, Dow-Jones & Company

g. Almost every industry has an industry periodical (such as *Progressive Grocer* in the supermarket business or *Advertising Age* in the advertising business). This would be a good source of information about issues facing the industry.

ON THE INTERNET: Alternatively, or in addition to your library search, you may want to "surf the net" for trends and developments affecting your company's industry. Go to the Baldwin homepage at **http://www.baldwin.swcollege.com,** select *The Financial Reporting Project*, and explore the hot links listed under Assignment 4.

COMPLETING THE ASSIGNMENT:

1. Use one or more sources from Category 1 to familiarize yourself with trends and developments within your chosen industry. (Do **not** use the Internet as a source of information for this portion of the assignment.)

   a. Which Category 1 source(s) did you consult? ______________________

   ____

   ____

   b. What major trends and developments are occurring in your industry? Summarize the information you obtained from Category 1 sources. Answer this question essay-style using complete sentences.

   ____

   ____

   ____

   ____

   ____

   ____

   ____

   ____

   ____

   ____

   ____

   ____

   ____

   ____

   ____

   ____

   ____

2. Use one or more of the Category 2 sources suggested above (or the Internet) to identify recent articles about your industry. Generally you should focus on articles that are no more than two years old. Select one recent article concerning your industry. Find the article, read it, and if you believe it conveys significant and interesting information, photocopy it to turn in with this assignment. If not, keep looking until you find such an article.

   Coordinate with your other group members to be sure that you do not duplicate articles. That is, each member of your group should evaluate a different article. For maximum benefit, each member of the group should provide a copy of his/her article to all the other group members.

   a. Index used to find the selected article: ______________________

   b. Citation for the article:

      i. Name of periodical ______________________

      ii. Title of article ______________________

      iii. Date of periodical ____________

      iv. Page numbers ________

   c. Article analysis: Describe and discuss why the information in the selected article is important to your industry? Limit your response to no more than 100 words and use complete sentences.

____

____

____

____

____

____

____

____

____

____

____

3. Attach photocopies of the articles to this assignment. Also, provide a copy of your article to each of your group members. (Note: It is a serious breach of academic integrity to tear articles out of magazines that do not belong to you...e.g., those in the library. Please don't do it!)

Reading 4

Monument Company Misjudges Funeral Industry, Pays with Its Life

THE BUSINESS:
Memorial-carving company
FOUNDED: 1947 **CLOSED:** 1996
PRIMARY CAUSE OF DEATH:
Failure to diversify as product demand waned
SECONDARY CAUSES OF DEATH: Lack of investment in technology and quality control

By PHAEDRA HISE

Peter Molina was dying to get into the booming funeral industry. In 1990 he bought Apperson & Dent, a monument-carving company in Alexandria, Va. Molina, a retired air-force officer with no experience in the industry, left operations to his son, Peter Molina Jr., then 34, who'd worked at Apperson & Dent on and off since 1984, and his son's brother-in-law, Mark Heddings, who'd worked at the company for 16 years. But the venture was doomed from the start. Although the funeral industry has thrived over the past six years, demand for upright markers from the country's 3,000 or so monument carving shops has slowed in the past decade.

One factor contributing to that decline is cemetery consolidation. The large management companies that are buying up small cemeteries slash maintenance costs by installing markers flush to the ground. The three largest cemeteries in Alexandria mandate flat markers. It's not surprising, then, that sales of flat marble and cast bronze markers are what's growing. But Apperson & Dent didn't diversify into that market. And the company's revenues, which in the mid-1980s had reached as high as $400,000, dwindled as cemeteries started selling their own monuments, some adding "installation" fees of up to $500 if customers purchased monuments elsewhere.

Peter Molina Sr. responded to fading revenues with several bad management decisions. He stopped restocking inventory, drastically reducing the samples from which customers could choose. He passed up a computerized system that would have saved labor costs by mapping designs on the stones. And he began outsourcing low-margin work, such as adding new names to previously installed headstones. That move proved fatal, as complaints about poor work began pouring in.

By 1992, when the first customer complaint was registered with the Better Business Bureau, Apperson & Dent was lucky to sell a monument a week. At the time, Heddings wasn't sure where the income was going. "We'd sell a monument for $2,000, take half down in cash, and then order a stone for $500." Apperson & Dent might spend another $350 to $500 on carving and installation. "But then we wouldn't pay the granite companies," Heddings says.

After too many complaints about unfinished work, Arlington National Cemetery finally quit referring customers to Apperson & Dent in 1995. Stones there had accounted for up to 65% of the company's revenues. "It killed them," says Heddings, who quit in 1992 to start his own monument-carving business. "In this market, once you lose Arlington, you might as well pack up."

In October 1996 Apperson & Dent filed for bankruptcy, owing three years of back taxes and leaving unhappy customers with loved ones resting in unmarked graves. Neither of the Molinas would return calls to discuss the company's closing.

"When the founders of Apperson & Dent were alive, I loved sending customers there," says Thomas Bowling of Ivy Hill Cemetery. "It was the best monument shop in the area. But it turned into a disaster."

Inc.
January 1997
Page 17

A **QUESTION FOR CONSIDERATION** appears on the next page.

QUESTION FOR CONSIDERATION:

Do you think Mr. Molina, Sr. made a bad decision when he decided to purchase this company? Why or why not?

Name: ______________________ Professor: ______________________

Course: ______________________ Section: ______________________

Assignment 5
INITIAL REVIEW OF ANNUAL REPORT AND FINANCIAL STATEMENTS

Name of your company: ______________________

By now you should have received the Annual Report (plus SEC 10-K and proxy statement) you requested from your company. The purpose of this assignment is to review and understand the basic information that is reported in your company's Annual Report with primary emphasis on the financial statements. The SEC 10-K and proxy statement are the focus of Assignment 6.

ORGANIZATION OF THE ANNUAL REPORT:

In general, Annual Reports are organized into the six different sections below.

1. *Financial Highlights:* In the first few pages or so you will find a summary of financial highlights covering as many as 10 or 20 years. Often this section contains a variety of charts and graphs. These data are not financial statements but merely a shorthand summary of the firm over many years.

2. *The Company And Its Products:* Near the beginning of the report there is usually a fairly lengthy section about the company and its products. (If the company has had a good year there will probably be lots of color pictures of the executives. If the company had a bad year they might leave out pictures of the executives altogether.) This section of the report includes mostly public relations-type information. It's a chance for the company to brag about its products, people and activities.

3. *Management Discussion And Analysis:* Following the public relations section of the Annual Report you will find a section titled "Management's Discussion and Analysis." Often this section is referred to in the business press by its initials: the MD&A. Here, management is required to identify significant events, trends and developments affecting the firm and to discuss management's thinking on these matters.

4. *Financial Statements and the Notes to the Financial Statements:* Following the MD&A you should find the financial statements and accompanying notes. Generally, there will be a balance sheet, income statement, statement of cash flows, and a statement of stockholders' equity. Often, each financial statement will have the word "Consolidated" in its title to indicate that the corporation owns one or more subsidiaries and that the financial results of the subsidiaries have been combined with those of the parent company to produce a single set of financial statements. The Notes are an integral part of the financial statements because they disclose the accounting methods used by the firm, provide detail regarding certain amounts on the face of the financial statements, and disclose additional matters not otherwise revealed by the financial statements. Financial statements without the accompanying notes comprise incomplete disclosure and can be misleading.

5. *Statement of Management Responsibility and the Report of the Independent Accountants* (or *Auditor's Report*): Read them carefully. These statements reveal (1) who is responsible for the content of the financial statements and (2) whether the financial statements present fairly the financial situation of the firm.

6. *Basic Company Facts:* Following the Notes to the Financial Statements there are usually two or three pages of basic facts about the company (e.g., list of officers and directors, stock exchange listing, state of incorporation).

COMPLETING THE ASSIGNMENT:

1. Read the Management Discussion and Analysis (MD&A) section. What is the general tone of management's comments in this section? Was the most recent year a positive or negative experience for the company? Does management appear optimistic or pessimistic about the future? Discuss.

2. The Income Statement

   a. Which format was used to prepare your firm's income statement? (Check one)

      Single-step ____

      Multiple-step ____

      > **HINT:** If gross margin (also called gross profit) is reported on the income statement, it's the multiple-step format. Otherwise, the single-step format has been used.

   b. Determine whether any of the following "special items" appear on the most recent income statement. They tend to appear near the bottom. Indicate below whether the item appears and (if it appears) indicate whether it increased or decreased net income. (These items will the subject of further analysis in a later assignment.)

	Item present?	**Increase or decrease?**
i. Discontinued operations	________	________
ii. Cumulative effect of a change in accounting principle	________	________
iii. Extraordinary gain (or loss)	________	________

   c. Using your judgment, list the **major** items of revenue and expense that are reported on your company's most recent income statement. For each item, indicate whether it is a revenue or an expense. Do not include any of the special items from Part b above.

	Revenue or expense?
i. ____________________________________	__________
ii. ____________________________________	__________
iii. ____________________________________	__________
iv. ____________________________________	__________
v. ____________________________________	__________
vi. ____________________________________	__________

3. The Balance Sheet

   a. Which of the following terms describes the balance sheet as reported by your firm? (Check those that apply.)

Classified balance sheet ____	(i.e., assets are segregated into categories)
Comparative balance sheet ____	(i.e., more than one year of data is presented)

   b. If your company presented a classified balance sheet, identify the amounts your firm reported for each of the following categories and the percentage of total assets that each represents.

	Amount	**Percent**
i. Current assets	________	______
ii. Property, plant, and equipment	________	______
iii. Other long-term assets	________	______
iv. Current liabilities	________	______
v. Long-term liabilities	________	______
vi. Contributed capital	________	______
vii. Retained earnings	________	______

> **LEARNING NOTE:** If you were a creditor of a firm (i.e., the firm owed you money) you would be interested in whether the firm had enough resources to pay you when your bill came due. Two indicators of a firm's ability to pay its bills as they become due are (1) the amount of working capital (sometimes called net working capital), and (2) the current ratio (sometimes called the working capital ratio).
>
> Working capital (WC) is the cushion by which total current assets exceed total current liabilities (*WC = current assets minus current liabilities*). The current ratio (CR) reveals how many dollars of current assets are available to pay off each dollar of current liabilities (*CR = current assets divided by current liabilities*).

c. What amount of working capital did your company have as of the date of its two most recent balance sheets? (Note: If your firm didn't prepare a classified balance sheet, you can't compute the amount of working capital or the current ratio. If that's the case, leave this page blank and skip to the next page.)

	Most Recent Balance Sheet	**Next Most Recent Balance Sheet**
Working capital	______	______

d. What was the current ratio, also known as the working capital ratio (current assets ÷ current liabilities), at the end of the two most recent years? For comparison to other firms, check with five classmates (who are analyzing different firms) to see what their results were. Record those results below along with those of your firm. List the names of each comparative firm.

	Most Recent Year	**Next Most Recent Year**
Your firm	______	______
______	______	______
______	______	______
______	______	______
______	______	______
______		______

e. How does your firm appear to compare to the other firms you listed above regarding its ability to pay current liabilities as they become due?

______

______

______

______

______

______

______

4. The Statement of Cash Flows

a. Which format does your company use to report the statement of cash flows? (check one)

Direct format	____	(The operating activities section begins with a line such as "Cash received from customers.")
Indirect format	____	(The operating activities section begins with a line such as "Net income" or "Net loss" and then proceeds to add and subtract items from that amount.)

b. In the spaces provided below, fill-in the proper summary amounts from your company's most recent statement of cash flows. If any category reports a net cash outflow, show that amount in parentheses.

i. Net cash inflow (outflow) from operating activities: ____________

ii. Net cash inflow (outflow) from financing activities: ____________

iii. Net cash inflow (outflow) from investing activities: ____________

iv. Net increase (decrease) in cash [or, sometimes labeled net change in cash and cash equivalents] for the year: ____________

c. Now go back to the balance sheet and fill-in the following amounts that are reported for Cash (under the assets category).

i. Current year's ending cash balance ____________

ii. Prior year's ending cash balance ____________

iii. Change in cash balance during the current year ____________

d. Does the number on line c.-iii. above match the number on line b.-iv. above? (check one below) Hint: They should match. This is an example of **financial statement articulation**, which means that numbers reported on one financial statement are related to numbers on the other statements.

i. Yes ____ No ____

ii. If the amounts do not match, by how much do they differ?

$______________

5. The Statement of Stockholders' Equity

   a. Did your company include a statement of stockholders' equity with the rest of its financial statements? (check one)

      Yes ___ No ___ (If no, ignore question b that follows.)

   b. Carefully review the most recent year's data on the statement of stockholders' equity. Were there any significant changes in the amounts comprising stockholders' equity between the beginning of the year and the end of the year? If so, complete the table below for the significant changes. In the right-most column, use parentheses to indicate a balance that decreased.

      Ignore changes that you judge to be insignificant. If your company had no significant changes in the amounts comprising stockholders' equity, note that on the first line of the table.

Statement of Stockholders' Equity Accounts	**Balance at Beginning of Year**	**Balance at End of Year**	**Change in Balance During Year**
______________________	________	________	________
______________________	________	________	________
______________________	________	________	________
______________________	________	________	________
______________________	________	________	________
______________________	________	________	________

6. "Articulation of Financial Statements" refers to information on one financial statement being related to information on another financial statement. Find an additional example of articulation in your company's financial statements beyond the example involving cash from part 4.-d. on the previous page. Describe it below.

____

____

____

____

____

Reading 5

Memory Lapse: How a Salesman Built Hottest Stock of 1996 Before the Roof Fell In

Now Centennial Technologies Is Restating Its 'Profits' And Mr. Pinez Is in Prison

Fine Product, if It Existed

By JON G. AUERBACII
Staff Reporter of The Wall Street Journal

Plymouth, Mass. — Emanuel Pinez sits slouched in his olive-green prison uniform, shifting a mug from hand to hand as he stares through the glass that separates prisoners from visitors at the Plymouth County Correctional Facility.

The former chief executive of Centennial Technologies Inc., awaiting trial on securities-fraud charges, scoffs at questions he is asked about his alleged wrongdoing. They "don't know what they're talking about" at the Securities and Exchange Commission, which investigated him along with federal prosecutors, Mr. Pinez says, predicting his vindication. Breaking into a smile, he adds, "Just you wait and see."

His quarters in Plymouth are more modest than the first-class accommodations Mr. Pinez has known in a long business career. But the man, many who know him say, remains essentially the same: confident, charming, never doubting he will prevail...and thoroughly compromising with the truth.

Led by Mr. Pinez, who has pleaded guilty, Centennial became a technology highflier. Its stock soared 451% last year as the top performer on the New York Stock Exchange. At a peak of $58.25 in December, the maker of memory cards for personal computers had a market value of more than $1 billion.

Today, kicked off the Big Board, Centennial is scrambling to right itself and says it expects to restate results from the time it went public in 1994, probably wiping out all reported profits. Having fired Mr. Pinez in February, it has hired a turnaround specialist, Lawrence J. Ramaekers, as interim chief executive. It is continuing to sell its PC cards, recently announcing a move to larger facilities. Its shares trade at about $3 in the unlisted "gray market" for over-the-counter stocks.

Insider Information

Federal prosecutors allege that Mr. Pinez padded Centennial's books with bogus sales. An indictment in federal court in Boston says he booked sales of one product that never even existed, then paid for orders with his own money to make them look real. Mr. Pinez built a paper fortune in Centennial stock — $240 million at one point — and then, the SEC says, used inside information to make a profitable play in the options market ahead of the stock plunge that came when the company announced his ouster.

The company says the alleged scam went undetected for three years by other managers as well as by its board, whose members include Bank of Boston chief financial officer William Shea and former Digital Equipment Corp. executive John J. Shields. Coopers & Lybrand, Centennial's auditor, and four brokerage houses that helped it raise almost $30 million evidently didn't catch anything, either.

Reports of improprieties and untruthful, even outlandish, claims have trailed Mr. Pinez throughout his life, including 30 years in business in Israel, Europe and the U.S. In a less-hectic stock market, lawyers and investment bankers say, underwriters might have done a thorough background search that could have raised red flags and prevented the Centennial debacle. But underwriters have been so busy, says Morton Pierce, a lawyer with Dewey Ballantine in New York, that they often rely exclusively on meetings with management for their information.

"I was absolutely surprised that nobody checked about his past," says Ariel Cohen, who is vice mayor of Jerusalem and has known Mr. Pinez for more than 30 years. Had people done so, Mr. Cohen says, they would have discovered a man known in Israel for his propensity to tell whoppers.

Channel Surfing

Born in Tel Aviv in 1938, Mr. Pinez says he studied geology and chemistry at Hebrew University. Although he later included a degree from the Jerusalem school on his resume, Mr. Pinez now concedes he didn't finish. "It looks much better if you say you graduated," he says.

In 1958, Mr. Pinez persuaded a now-defunct Israeli magazine, Haolam Hazeh, to send him to France for a swimming race across the English Channel. He then cabled the magazine from the Israeli embassy in Paris saying he had won and set a world record, crossing the channel in 10 hours and 21 minutes, says Uri Avnery, who was the magazine's longtime editor. Haolam Hazeh published the remarkable tale, and Mr. Pinez was hailed briefly as a national hero.

Several weeks later, after doubts raised in the French press, it came out that there was no record of the race's ever having taken place. The embarrassed magazine printed a two-page retraction, describing its first report as the "most curious" crossing of a body of water since Moses and the Israelites traversed the Red Sea. "The whole thing became a complete laughingstock," the editor says. Just recently, the channel tale was recounted in the Israeli weekly Kol Ha'ir.

Mr. Pinez spent six months studying computers in London in 1967, and he later said in public filings that he had received a master's degree from the London School of Economic EF. He now concedes that claim, too, was false.

Several former colleagues, among them accountant Charles Badenoch, say Mr. Pinez often boasted that he was a paratrooper in the Israeli army during the 1967 Six Day War. Mr. Pinez acknowledges he never fought in the war, but denies ever saying he had.

Rachel Pinez, Mr. Pinez's wife of 36 years, calls her husband a "pathological liar," attributing his ways to a need to come out on top. "You can call it imagination or you can call it lying, but he does it to prove he's smarter than everyone else," says Mrs. Pinez, who lives in Switzerland. She also says, and Mr. Pinez confirms, that for three years he concealed from her his relationship with a woman in the U.S.

In 1968, the Pinezes moved from Israel to Geneva, where Mr. Pinez teamed up with an associate to launch Indur, a computer-services company acquired in 1970 by Sisco, a unit of Singer Co. But Mr. Pinez was fired by Indur in 1971 after a suspicious Sisco executive raided his Swiss office one night and discovered phony invoices in a drawer, according to two former officials of the company, including Kurt Miersch, a former Sisco director. The invoices had never been sent out, but corresponding amounts of sales had been booked by Sisco, Mr. Miersch says.

Made aware of this account, Mr. Pinez initially says he was fired because he "refused to buy [Mr. Miersch] a comfortable chair." Later in the interview, he acknowledges there had been "Some invoices that I had a difficulty with collectibility. "

After a brief stint running another Geneva computer concern, Mr. Pinez and two associates launched ABL Technologies Ltd., which sold ink ribbons and golf ball shaped print wheels, then in high demand for computer printers. ABL took off. Splitting his time between company offices in Geneva, London and Los Angeles, colleagues say, Mr. Pinez lived a comfortable life of top hotels, fancy cars and expensive wines. Joan Campbell, a former accounting vice president at ABL's U.S. unit, says Mr. Pinez once gave her a tongue-lashing for booking him in a hotel room with a shower but no tub, and he demanded a suite with a kitchen so he could prepare two soft-boiled eggs each morning.

Some former ABL employees say that between 1982 and 1985. Mr. Pinez ordered them to wire U.S. profits of up to $50,000 a week to company bank accounts in London, Geneva and Jersey, the tax haven off the English coast. Mrs. Campbell says that when accounting for internal transfers, the company's European operations retroactively inflated prices charged to the U.S. unit so profits didn't appear on the U.S. books. She says Mr. Pinez told her ABL didn't want to keep the money in the U.S., to avoid paying U.S. taxes. Mr. Pinez won't comment — except. to say he "wasn't involved in any finances" at ABL.

Mrs. Campbell also says Mr. Pinez told her several times that he was on the board of directors of Hewlett-Packard Co. Hewlett-Packard says he never was. Through his lawyer, Mr. Pinez had no comment.

In 1983, Mr. Pinez recruited Donald Carroll, who had been dean of the University of Pennsylvania's Wharton School, as ABL's chairman. Mr. Carroll left about six months later after an argument in which he accused Mr. Pinez of infringing on other manufacturers' patents, according to people familiar with the events. Linda Ory, a former ABL sales executive, says ABL was sued frequently for patent infringements, often agreeing to pay royalties when they were discovered. Mr. Pinez says he doesn't remember a confrontation with Mr. Carrol, but "if there were any... infringements, it was settled."

In 1986, Mr. Pinez resigned from ABL. It filed for receivership the next year.

Setag and Setag

Mr. Pinez surfaced in Massachusetts in 1987 at the helm of a start-up company that sold font cartridges for printers. He called it Setag Inc., nearly identical to Setag SA, a Swiss company that was his print-wheel supplier.

Nicole Koval, the daughter of Setag SA's late founder George Ceppi, says that the Swiss company never authorized the use of its name, and that after a period, Mr. Pinez fell behind in payments. She says Setag SA hired a lawyer to help it get the money, but Mr. Pinez was buying the products through a Swiss-based company that filed for bankruptcy in 1989, making recovery impossible.

Mr. Pinez later changed Setag Inc.'s name to Centennial, and in April 1991 he took it public. Leading the $4.7 million initial offering were underwriters Nutmeg Securities Ltd. of Westport, Conn., and Schneider Securities Inc. of Denver. T.J. O'Rourke, an owner of Schneider, says his firm did an "extensive" background check but won't say what it found. Matthew Rochlin, Nutmeg's president, says he doesn't remember what kind of background check was done.

Mr. Pinez quickly began making upbeat growth estimates and hinting of big contracts to come. Centennial often issued news releases heralding "record" orders or reporting new orders with dollar amounts, but no names of the buyers. Revenues and profits were small but rising fast, more than 150% in some quarters. The stock soared.

Talk Of a Big Contract

In early 1996, at a time when the company's most recent reported annual revenue was $12.4 million, Mr. Pinez began telling institutional investors Centennial was negotiating for AT&T Corp. to pay it up to $300 million for a system to track truck fleets by satellite. Tom Pence, a portfolio manager with Conseco Capital Management in Carmel, Ind., says he began buying Centennial shares last May after Mr. Pinez told him he was close to sealing the AT&T deal. Bart Epker, a partner with PAR Capital Management in Boston, says Mr. Pinez told him about a likely AT&T deal in early August. AT&T has declined to comment, and no agreement has been announced.

At about the same time, Mr. Pinez also began boosting Centennial's revenues and profits by creating a fictitious product called "Flash 98," the federal indictment alleges. It says he assigned his creation, ostensibly a miniature memory card, a per-unit cost of 10 cents and a price of $500 — which meant that "sales" were almost pure profit.

During calendar 1996, Centennial booked $2.1 million in sales of Flash 98 cards. The indictment says, the Centennial records show the buyer as BBC Computers Inc., a New Hampshire-based unit of Presage Corp. of Woburn, Mass. Presage is run by Robert E. Lockwood, who Mr. Pinez says is a close friend.

According to the federal indictment, Mr. Pinez then wired more than $1 million of his own funds to a third company, which in turn paid Centennial on behalf of BBC.

In a matter not involving Centennial, Mr. Lockwood was indicted last week by a state grand jury in Suffolk County, Mass., on 13 counts of tax-evasion related to his companies. He didn't return phone calls seeking comment.

More Stock

As Centennial prepared for a second, $22.8 million stock issue in March 1996 managed by Needham & Co. and Furman Selz LLC, Mr. Pinez toured the country talking to investors. At a stop in Boston, he laid out a strategy for building a global network of low-cost contract manufacturers.

Following the issue, recommendations by analysts from the underwriters and news releases citing new orders moved the stock upward, attracting some big mutual funds. In April 1996, John Hancock Advisers Inc.'s Emerging Growth Fund bought 25,000 Centennial shares, according to Technimetrics Inc., a New York research firm. In July, Oppenheimer Funds Inc. snapped up 360,000 shares for its Capital Appreciation and Global Securities funds. Fidelity Investments' Select Electronics Portfolio fund bought 198,600 shares in August.

But some investors started to crave a first-hand look. Conseco sent analyst Mark Babka to meet with Mr. Pinez last July at Centennial's headquarters in Billerica, north of Boston. Mr. Babka says he began to worry when Mr. Pinez and another executive gave him financial estimates sharply lower than previous ones.

And although Centennial made computer equipment, Mr. Babka says, he noticed there was no computer in Mr. Pinez's office other than a small digital organizer he opened and closed throughout the meeting.

During a tour of manufacturing facilities, Mr. Babka says, he expected to see high-tech machinery churning out credit card-size memory cards. Instead, "there was a room full of people banging on cards with rubber mallets. I had a bad feeling." Conseco dumped its shares.

Buyers and Sellers

By now, the stock had gained the attention of "momentum" investors who buy stocks that have been appreciating rapidly. The Cabot Market Letter, a Salem, Mass., publication followed by the momentum crowd, began urging investors to load up on Centennial in November, and sister company Cabot Money Management began accumulating 222,618 shares for its investors. The stock reached $55 before a two-for-one split at the end of November, and then quickly doubled, climbing to a high of $58.25 on Dec. 30. Many of the mutual-fund managers got out during this period.

Besides the buyers, skeptical investors were shorting the stock, that is, betting on a decline by selling borrowed shares. And at Centennial's annual meeting in early November, Mr. Pinez was asked point-blank about the AT&T deal but declined to comment, people who were there say.

Mr. Pinez often boasted that he never sold any of his Centennial shares. But he used about 3.5 million of his 4.2 million shares as collateral to borrow a total of $18.5 million from Lehman Brothers Inc. and PaineWebber Inc., according to the SEC. Some of those borrowed funds were used to pay for sales of Flash 98, the indictment alleges.

Mr. Pinez also gave away 703,765 shares, unadjusted for splits, as gifts between 1994 and 1996, according to federal filings — shares that were worth about $21 million when given. He had to tell Centennial the names of the recipients and attest that he wasn't linked to them. Now Centennial says it is investigating whether Mr. Pinez later benefited from the gifts. It won't identify the recipients. Through an attorney, Mr. Pinez, declines to discuss the gifts.

Four days before he was fired, the indictment says, Mr. Pinez placed orders for 5,400 option contracts betting that Centennial stock would fall. The proceeds of those transactions, which have been frozen by federal-judge in Boston, exceeded $4 million. With the stock down 90% from its high, Centennial now faces shareholder lawsuits.

In Plymouth, where he sits awaiting trial, Mr. Pinez interrupts an interview with frequent bouts of coughing, the remnant of past heavy smoking. He attributes his problems to the scrutiny that inevitably comes with success. "You get lightning when you're very high," he says.

The Wall Street Journal
April 11, 1997
Page A1

QUESTIONS FOR CONSIDERATION:

1. What lessons can be learned from the Centennial Technologies scam?
2. If you had been an investor in Centennial Technologies when it collapsed, would you be angry at anyone besides Mr. Pinez? Who? Why?

Author's Note: In June of 1997, the company restated its financial statements for the 14 quarters through the end of 1996. It disclosed losses totaling $28.1 million and reported that it never had a profitable quarter during that period. At the beginning of 1998, Mr. Pinez still sits in jail awaiting trial. The stock has been delisted from all organized exchanges, but trades on the "gray market" at about $1.50 per share. The company continues to limp along, has new management, is reporting losses, but "hope springs eternal" among some investors still holding shares .

Name: ______________________ Professor: ______________

Course: ______________________ Section: ______________

Assignment 6
THE SEC 10-K REPORT AND PROXY STATEMENT

The Securities and Exchange Commission (SEC), an agency of the federal government, was established by the Securities Exchange Act of 1934. Its primary function is to promote full-disclosure of all material financial facts and other information concerning securities offered for public sale. The SEC does not prevent the sale of risky or low-quality securities but, instead, strives to make sure that investors are fully informed as to nature of the investment they are making.

The purpose of this assignment is for you to understand the similarities and differences between a company's Annual Report to Shareholders and its SEC Form 10-K which must be submitted to the Securities and Exchange Commission (SEC) annually. In addition, you will review your firm's proxy statement and evaluate certain information from it.

Name of your company: ______________________________

In general, companies having assets of $1 million or more and 500 or more stockholders are subject to SEC regulation if their securities (e.g., stocks or bonds) are traded publicly. Principal among those regulations is the filing of regular public reports with the Commission. While there are more than a dozen different reporting forms used by SEC registrants, the three most commonly used reporting documents are the SEC Form:

a. 10-Q (the quarterly report to the SEC)

b. 8-K (an irregular report of unscheduled events or corporate changes important to shareholders or the SEC. For example, when a company changes independent auditors it must publicly announce that event by filing an 8-K with the SEC.)

c. 10-K (the annual report to the SEC)

The 10-K is, by far, the best known of the SEC-required reports. In essence, it is a special version of the company's Annual Report. In this assignment you will learn how these are similar and how these are different. You will also discover that interesting information is disclosed in the proxy statement.

> **ON THE INTERNET:** Since 1996, the SEC has required all public companies to make their required SEC filings (e.g., 10-Qs, 8-Ks, 10-Ks) electronically. These filings are then posted to the SEC's web site within 24 hours. This system is called EDGAR which stands for Electronic Data Gathering, Analysis, and Retrieval. You can access EDGAR by going to the Baldwin homepage at **http://www.baldwin.swcollege.com**, selecting *The Financial Reporting Project,* and using the information listed under Assignment 6.

COMPLETING THE ASSIGNMENT:

The outline of this assignment is as follows. First, you are to identify each of the required sections of the SEC 10-K and indicate where they appear in your company's report. Second, you are asked to assess the similarities and differences between the information contained in your company's SEC 10-K and its Annual Report. Third, you are asked to record certain specific information about your company that is disclosed on the proxy statement.

1. The SEC 10-K Report is comprised of 14 items organized into four parts as shown below. Review your company's SEC Form 10-K and note the page(s) where each item is reported.

		Page(s) Where Item is Reported
PART I:		
Item 1.	Business	____________
Item 2.	Properties	____________
Item 3.	Legal Proceedings	____________
Item 4.	Submission of Matters to Vote of Security Holders	____________
PART II:		
Item 5.	Market for the Registrant's Common Equity and Related Stockholder Matters	____________
Item 6.	Selected Financial Data	____________

Item 7.	Management's Discussion and Analysis of Financial Condition and Results of Operations	__________
Item 8.	Financial Statements and Supplementary Data	__________
Item 9.	Changes in and Disagreements with Accountants on Accounting and Financial Disclosure	__________
PART III:		
Item 10.	Directors and Executive Officers of the Registrant	__________
Item 11.	Executive Compensation	__________
Item 12.	Security Ownership of Certain Beneficial Owners and Management	__________
Item 13.	Certain Relationships and Related Transactions	__________
PART IV:		
Item 14.	Exhibits, Financial Statement Schedules, and Reports on Form 8-K	__________

2. After carefully comparing your firm's annual report to its SEC 10-K, answer the following questions. What information did you find in both the annual report and the SEC 10-K? What information is contained in one document that is not contained in the other. Why do you think these differences exist? Answer these questions essay-style using complete sentences.

____

____

____

____

____

____

____

____

3. Answer the following questions based on information disclosed in the proxy statement.

   a. Identify the date and location of the stockholders' meeting announced in the proxy statement.

      i. Date ______________

      ii. Location ____

   b. Briefly describe the proposals, issues, or topics that were scheduled for action at the stockholders' meeting.

   ____

   ____

   ____

   ____

   ____

   c. For your firm's highest paid executive, compute the total dollar amount of compensation (e.g., salary + bonus + etc.) that he/she received from the company in each of the last three years.

      For perspective about how your firm's highest paid executive compares to those of other firms, check with five classmates (who are studying different firms than you) and record their information below also. To conserve space, record information in thousands of dollars (000's).

Highest Paid Executive's Total Compensation	Your Firm	CLASSMATES' FIRMS Firm 1	Firm 2	Firm 3	Firm 4	Firm 5
i. Most recent year	______	______	______	______	______	______
ii. Next most recent year	______	______	______	______	______	______
iii. Next most recent year	______	______	______	______	______	______

d. How does the total compensation of your firm's highest-paid executive compare to the highest-paid executives of your classmates' firms over the past three years? Discuss.

e. Inspect the stock performance graph near the end of the proxy statement. How does the price performance of the company's stock compare to that of other companies? Does the trend in stock returns match the trend in compensation being earned by the company's top executives? Discuss.

Name: ______________________ Professor: ______________________

Course: ______________________ Section: ______________________

Assignment 7
THE ACCOUNTING PROFESSION

The purpose of this assignment is to learn about the independent accounting firm that audited your company's financial statements. You will have an opportunity to further develop your library research skills. (Make no mistake about it, these skills are valued by employers. They expect you to know how to find business information about potential customers, suppliers, competitors, or firms that might be potential acquisitions.)

KEY REFERENCES FOR THIS ASSIGNMENT:

Category 1 Sources:

a. *Directory of Leading Private Companies*, National Register Publishing Company

b. *Million Dollar Directory*, Dun & Bradstreet (volumes labeled "America's Leading Public & Private Companies)

Category 2 Sources:

a. *ABI-Inform*, UMI, Inc (on CD-ROM)

b. *Accountants Index*, American Institute of Certified Public Accountants

c. *Business Newsbank*, Newsbank, Inc. (on CD-ROM)

d. *Business Periodicals Index*, H.W. Wilson Company

e. *Predicast F&S Index*, Predicasts

f. *The New York Times Index*, New York Times Company

g. *The Wall Street Journal Index*, Dow-Jones & Company

COMPLETING THE ASSIGNMENT:

1. Name of your company: ______________________________

2. Name of your company's auditor: ______________________________

3. Size of the Accounting Firm

The purpose of this section is to demonstrate that the public accounting firms that audit large U.S. companies are, generally, very large companies themselves. The "Big Six" accounting firms (Arthur Andersen, Coopers & Lybrand, Deloitte and Touche, Ernst and Young, KPMG Peat Marwick, and Price Waterhouse) all had revenues in 1996 of between $2.0 and $4.5 billion dollars. Odds are, your firm was audited by one of these companies.

Use either of the Category 1 "Key References" to determine the following information about your firm's independent auditor. If your library does not have either of these references, the Reference Librarian probably can suggest alternative sources from which to obtain the data.

> **ON THE INTERNET:** The information needed below is usually included at the accounting firm's website, although you may have to hunt for it some. You can access your auditor's website by going to the Baldwin homepage at **http://www.baldwin.swcollege.com.** Select *The Financial Reporting Project*, select Assignment 7, and click on the button of your firm's auditor.

a. Where is the home office of your company's auditor? ________________

b. How many employees does the accounting firm have?

____

Indicate, in the space provided below, whether this is the number of U.S. employees, employees world-wide, or whether this cannot be determined from the information source used. Also, indicate the year to which this information pertains.

______________________________ Year ______

c. What is the annual sales revenue of the accounting firm that audited your corporation? Indicate the year to which this information pertains.

$________________ Year ______

4. Current Issues Facing Your Company's Independent Auditor

Use one or more of the Category 2 "Key References" (or the Internet) to identify recent articles about your company's independent auditor. Generally, focus on articles that are no more than two year's old. Select two recent articles concerning your firm's auditor (no more than one article from a single index). Find articles that you believe convey significant and interesting information. Photocopy them to turn in with this assignment.

a. Index used to find article #1 ______________________________

b. Citation for article #1:

i. Name of periodical ______________________________

ii. Title of article ______________________________

iii. Date of periodical ______________

iv. Page numbers __________

c. Article analysis: Why is this article significant and interesting? Limit your response to no more than 100 words and use complete sentences.

____

____

____

____

____

____

____

____

____

____

____

____

____

____

d. Index Used to Find Article #2______________________________

e. Citation for article #2:

i. Name of periodical ______________________________

ii. Title of article______________________________

iii. Date of periodical ____________

iv. Page numbers ________

f. Article analysis: Why is this article significant and interesting? Limit your response to no more than 100 words and use complete sentences.

5. Attach photocopies of the articles to this assignment. (Note: It is a serious breach of academic integrity to tear articles out of magazines that do not belong to you...i.e., those in the library. Please don't do it!)

Reading 7

Ernst & Young, Royal Dutch/Shell Unit To Form Accounting-Services Company

By A. Craig Copetas
And Elizabeth MacDonald
Staff Reporters of The Wall Street Journal

Paris – **Ernst & Young LLP** is expected to announce today a joint venture with oil giant Shell International Ltd., a unit of **Royal Dutch/Shell Group**, to create a partnership of superbookkeepers.

The new unit, Tasco Europe LLP, is a bold twist on the ideas of outsourcing. Every large company relies on outside auditors from accounting firms to check whether its internal auditors are working effectively to deter fraud and waste. But a growing number of companies are cutting costs by outsourcing their accounting and internal-audit departments to accounting firms. The total global accounting-outsourcing market will top $280 billion by 2000, with annual growth rates of 20% thereafter, according to G2 Research, a market-research firm in Mountain View, Calif.

"Tasco will initially do all of the accounting for affiliated Shell companies within the oil-products division of Shell International," said Jacky Ross, a partner in the Pan European shared service practice for Ernst & Young in London. "We're going to target other multinational companies around Europe who feel they can't handle this work on their own."

Ms. Ross, who will be the CEO of Tasco, added, "Many companies in the 1,000 largest global companies have expressed interest in buying accounting transaction services on a pan-European basis from one outlet." She estimated the size "of that market is around $1 billion."

Breaking Ground

To be sure, Tasco's experiment in outsourcing breaks ground in Europe as it's the first time a major accounting firm has created a joint venture with a multinational corporation to establish a pan-European accounting-services company. Shell International is a 50% partner in this new firm, but neither group would disclose the new venture's capitalization.

Worried about slumping audit revenues, the Big Six accounting firms say they have tripled in the past five years the amount of outsourcing work they perform. (If partners and regulators approve two large pending accounting-industry mergers, there will be just four main accounting firms. Price Waterhouse and Coopers & Lybrand have announced plans to merge as have Ernst & Young and KPMG Peat Marwick.)

Indeed, Price Waterhouse LLP recently signed a letter of intent to negotiate a takeover of Mobil Exploration & Producing U.S. Inc.'s entire U.S. accounting operation in a 10-year deal valued at several hundreds of millions of dollars, partners there say. If the deal goes through, Price will assume the day-to-day accounting and financial reporting for the company. Partners at Price Waterhouse expect the venture to be staffed with about 200 Mobil employees and about 30 Price staffers.

But regulatory experts say the Tasco venture may be rife with conflicts of interest. In addition, the new partnership will have to navigate through the rocky shoals of varying audit regulations from country to country.

Navigating Regulations

According to generally accepted auditing standards in Britain, for instance, accountants frown upon auditing their own work, though the procedure is legal, regulators there say. Accountants in the U.S. and France can't audit their own bookkeeping for client companies. The U.S. Securities and Exchange Commission has let the industry handle outsourcing on its own without regulatory intervention, so long as the firms don't use the same accountants who do the outsourcing to audit their work at the company. But SEC regulators are increasingly scrutinizing such deals, due to growing concerns that they could harm the integrity of financial statements and put shareholders at risk.

Dennis Beresford, the former chairman of the Financial Accounting Standards Board in the U. S., said in an interview, "I have some concerns about whether auditors are truly being fair and objective when they do accounting for a client while at the same time they audit the client's books." He added: "There are good business opportunities here for the industry, but accountants would be better off not doing it for their clients."

European Union auditing directives require auditing firms to be independent of the accountants corporations use to assemble their books. But EU officials say each member state in the 15-nation union is allowed to interpret the directives as they please. In general, respective state regulators require corporations to show that the individuals conducting corporate audits aren't the same people who did the accounting for that company.

Ms. Ross maintains the new company won't violate any auditing rules because Shell International isn't an audit client of Ernst & Young. However, Ms. Ross admits that Ernst & Young does conduct a "very limited amount of audit work for smaller units of Shell International in emerging markets." In a separate statement on the issue of independence, the company said the joint venture is "with the U.K. and U.S. firms of Ernst & Young. The French practices of Ernst & Young are not part of the joint venture, and the report on the Shell entities it audits are not included in any SEC filing."

Roger Mills-Hicks, the director of Shell's European accounting-services project, will serve as Tasco's chairman. The firm will employ approximately 200 new workers by the end of 1998, and some 1,200 people by 2002. Possible sites for the group's headquarters include the United Kingdom and the Netherlands.

The Wall Street Journal
October 31, 1997
Page B11F

QUESTIONS FOR CONSIDERATION:

1. Why do you think that U.S. and French regulations prohibit accounting firms from auditing their own bookkeeping work? How do the British view this practice? Identify and discuss the problems that might arise when accountants audit companies for which they also provide bookkeeping work.

2. Accounting firms often sell consulting services to the firms they audit. This is allowed under U.S. regulations. How do these two situations differ such that one practice is acceptable and the other isn't? Explain why you agree or disagree that these situations should be treated differently.

Name: ______________________ Professor: ______________________

Course: ______________________ Section: ______________________

Assignment 8
THE INCOME STATEMENT

Name of your company ______________________

The purpose of this assignment is to obtain an in-depth understanding of your company's income statement as shown in the annual report and SEC 10-K. Information will be reviewed regarding revenues, expenses, income taxes, "special items," and subsequent events. In addition, you will conduct a basic financial analysis of the income statement.

COMPLETING THE ASSIGNMENT:

1. Summarize the basic information on your company's income statements for the most recent three years. If an item was not reported, indicate by placing N.A. (for not applicable) in the space provided.

Basic Income Statement Information	**Most Recent Year**	**Next Most Recent Year**	**Second Most Recent Year**
a. Sales [or total revenues]	________	________	________
b. Cost of goods sold (CGS)	________	________	________
c. Gross margin [or gross profit or gross income]	________	________	________
d. Total other expenses, gains, and losses (other than CGS)	________	________	________
e. Income (loss) before taxes	________	________	________
f. Income taxes	________	________	________
g. Net income (loss)	________	________	________
h. Comprehensive income*	________	________	________

*This might be reported on a separate schedule rather than on the face of the income statement.

2. Identify any "special items" that appear on the income statements. Special items are comprised of (1) *income (or loss) from discontinued operations*, (2) *extraordinary gain (or loss)*, and (3) *cumulative effect of a change in accounting principle*. They are often referred to as "non-recurring items" because they are not expected to happen again. If any of these appeared on any of the income statements for the last three years, indicate the year and the amount and explain the underlying event/transaction that caused the item to arise. (Hint: These events usually are explained in the Notes to the Financial Statements.)

   a. Income (or loss) from discontinued operations:

   b. Extraordinary gain (or loss):

   c. Cumulative effect of a change in accounting principle:

3. In the Notes to the Financial Statements there should be a section with a title such as "Income Taxes." Read that note carefully before completing the following section.

   a. What is the federal tax rate on corporations (often called the *statutory tax rate*)? ______

   b. What *effective tax rate* (sometimes referred to as the *actual tax rate*) did your firm pay? ______

   c. If the firm's *effective* or *actual tax rate* was different from the *federal* or *statutory rate*, list up to three items that caused them to differ.

      ____

      ____

      ____

   d. What was the firm's total income tax expense (in dollars) for the most recent year? ____________

   > **LEARNING NOTE:** Deferred taxes usually are tax liabilities that will be paid on profits the company has reported on its income statement but that don't need to be paid to the government until some future date. (Sometimes, deferred taxes represent taxes that have been paid ahead of time. In that case they are reported as assets.)

   e. Did the amount of your company's deferred taxes increase or decrease during the most recent year? ____________

   f. By what amount did deferred taxes change from the prior year?

      ____

   g. List up to three examples of temporary differences that caused your firm to report deferred taxes.

      ____

      ____

      ____

> **LEARNING NOTE:** A subsequent event is a significant event or transaction that occurs after the balance sheet date but before the annual report is distributed (e.g., the obtaining of a large contract or an unfavorable result from a major lawsuit). Failure to disclose this type of event could render the financial statements misleading.

4. Did your firm disclose any subsequent events? (They usually are reported in the notes to the financial statements.) If so, briefly describe them below.

> **LEARNING NOTE:** To determine a company's profitability trends, a percentage analysis of successive years' income statements is often prepared. This analysis frequently is referred to as preparation of *common-size income statements.* In addition, profit margins usually are computed and compared to the profit margin data of other firms.
>
> On a common-size income statement, each item is expressed as a percentage of net sales revenue. Sales revenue is arbitrarily set to equal 100% and everything else is related to it. For example, if cost of goods sold were $300 and sales were $400, cost of goods sold would be listed on the common-size income statement as 75% ($300/$400). Every item on the income statement is divided by sales. This type of statement will reveal specific trends in revenue and expense items across the years that otherwise would be obscured by growing (or decreasing) sales.

5. Prepare a percentage analysis (*common-size income statements*) for the most recent three years. Special items, such as discontinued operations, extraordinary items, and cumulative effects are not included in the analysis because they are not expected to recur. Be sure to indicate the year of each column below. Put the most recent year's data in the left-most column.

   a. Complete the table below.

Income Statement Item	**Most Recent Year (% of sales)**	**Next Most Recent Year (% of sales)**	**Next Most Recent Year (% of sales)**
Sales revenue	100%	100%	100%
Cost of goods sold	______	______	______
Gross margin	______	______	______
Operating expenses:			
(1) ____________________	______	______	______
(2) ____________________	______	______	______
(3) ____________________	______	______	______
(4) ____________________	______	______	______
Total operating expenses	______	______	______
Operating income	______	______	______
Other (non-operating) revenues, expenses, gains, and losses:			
(1) ____________________	______	______	______
(2) ____________________	______	______	______
(3) ____________________	______	______	______
Income before income taxes	______	______	______
Provision for income taxes	______	______	______
Income before special items (such as discontinued operations, extraordinary items, or cumulative effect)	______	______	______

b. From the information in part (a) on the previous page, identify the significant data points or trends that you observe over the three years.

____

____

____

____

____

____

____

____

____

____

____

____

____

____

____

____

6. a. Summarize your firm's profit margins that you computed in Part 5a for each of the last three years. Indicate the year for each column and put the most recent year in the left-most column.

	Most Recent Year	**Next Most Recent Year**	**Next Most Recent Year**
i. Gross profit margin % (gross margin/sales revenue)	______	______	______
ii. Operating profit margin % (operating income/sales revenue)	______	______	______
iii. Net profit margin % (net income/sales revenue)	______	______	______

b. For perspective, compare your company's profit margins for the most recent year to those computed by classmates for their firms' most recent year.

	Your Firm	CLASSMATES' FIRMS Firm 1	Firm 2	Firm 3	Firm 4	Firm 5
i. Gross profit margin %	_____	_____	_____	_____	_____	_____
ii. Operating profit margin %	_____	_____	_____	_____	_____	_____
iii. Net profit margin %	_____	_____	_____	_____	_____	_____

c. How do your firm's margins compare to those of your classmates' firms? Are they high, low, or about the same? Is there anything specific about your firm, its industry, or your classmates' companies or industries that would tend to explain the differences between your company's margins and those of the other firms? Discuss. Also, how would you describe the trend in your company's margins over the past three years?

7. Other common measures of the profitability are the return on assets and return on equity. They are measures of efficiency that compare net income to the amount of assets and equity used to generate that income. The higher the returns, the more efficient was the use of assets and equity.

   a. Compute your firm's return on assets and return on equity for the most recent year using the following formulas. (Note: The exact formulas used to compute these ratios vary slightly among financial analysts.)

Return on assets = net income / average total assets*	**Return on equity** = net income / average stockholders' equity*

*[(beginning balance + ending balance)/2]

Return on assets = ______________________ = ______

Return on equity = ______________________ = ______

   b. Compare your company's returns to those of your classmates' firms.

	Your Firm	**CLASSMATES' FIRMS** Firm 1	**Firm 2**	**Firm 3**	**Firm 4**	**Firm 5**
Return on assets	_____	_____	_____	_____	_____	_____
Return on equity	_____	_____	_____	_____	_____	_____

   c. Assume this year's returns are representative of normal results. Do you think your company is an attractive investment? Discuss.

____

____

____

____

____

Reading 8

Growth Companies Feel Pressure to Book Sales

By GREG IP
Staff Reporter of The Wall Street Journal

It's nail-biting time again in growth-stock country.

As another quarter draws toward an end, officials at technology and other high-flying companies are getting anxious about meeting sales targets, while savvy customers are turning up the pressure for discounts. Both sides know that if just a few sales fail to close by the quarter's end, a company may fall short of hitting analysts' earnings estimates. That, in turn, could trigger a big plunge in the company's stock price.

"Customers know that the vendor needs to get the deal done by the end of the quarter to satisfy Street expectations, and they use that as a powerful negotiating tool," says James Smith, a portfolio manager at Pilgrim Baxter & Associates. "'OK, you want our $2 million order and you want to ship it by the end of June? Fine, we can make that happen for you, but this is what it will take: an additional 15% discount, or better shipping terms.' Customers have become very, very sophisticated in how to use their leverage because of the financial markets."

All that makes the closing weeks of a financial quarter more stressful than usual for growth companies – those with higher-than-average expected earnings growth – particularly smaller companies, for which each order is critical, and for the analysts who follow them. Often, more than 50% and as much as 75% of such companies' sales comes in the last month of the quarter, producing a "hockey stick" sales pattern. Management may not know until late whether it will meet Wall Street estimates. That contributes to the burst of negative profit warnings and stock carnage around a quarter's end.

"The joke in Silicon Valley for years has been, the chief financial officer calls the shipping dock at noon on the last day of the quarter and says, 'How did we do?' and the answer is, 'I don't know, the quarter is only half over,'" relates Thomas Thornhill, director of technology research at Montgomery Securities Inc.

"It produces stress for everybody," adds John Rossi, a technology analyst at Robertson Stephens & Co. "Late snafus, shortage of components, or sudden wavering by a customer could have a huge impact on the quarterly results. Suddenly out of nowhere comes this surprise shortfall, and that's when you get the mind-spinning drops in stock prices."

Technology companies are especially vulnerable to last-minute pressure tactics by customers because they are so closely followed by Wall Street.

"We encourage our clients to wait as long in the quarter as possible to make a purchase," says Jim Seay, research director at the Gartner Group, which advises major purchasers of technology. "Companies who don't make their earnings forecast are punished terribly, so that pressure flows down through the entire chain of command on the vendor side. The deal window opens the first or second week of the third month of the quarter."

The problem is most acute for companies with a relatively small number of customers, such as IKOS Systems Inc., Cupertino, Calif., which makes expensive simulation systems for electronics manufacturers; its 10 largest customers typically account for more than half the sales in a quarter.

"You have to spend a lot of time with each individual account, and you miss a couple of those, and it gets pretty ugly in a hurry," says IKOS's chief financial officer, Joseph Rockom. "We had a couple we thought we could get [in the second quarter] and they slipped out," though he blames customer-specific issues rather than negotiating tactics. That played a part in IKOS warning in early July that revenue would be less than expected, sending its stock down $5.25, or 26%, to $15.125 in one day.

The customer, he adds, "knows these high-tech companies are all trying to make their quarter and all of them are kind of on the hairy edge, so if [the supplier] needs another order to make the quarter, he's going to be a lot more receptive to negotiations." He says that though IKOS doesn't discount heavily, "if we need [the sale] to make the quarter, we'll do what we need to get it."

Mr. Rockom notes the customer faces pressure to close as well because it knows the leverage is gone once the quarter is over and the supplier is back in the driver's seat.

The late-quarter pressure is more often implicit than explicit, and originates on both sides, analysts say. Keith Mullins, a stock strategist at Smith Barney Inc., says, "I've seen cases where the companies have [said] to customers, 'We need to make a quarter, take some extra product.'"

Avid Technology Inc., a Tewksbury, Mass., developer of computer editing systems for broadcast, movies and video, failed to complete some expected sales in the last quarter of 1995. It warned in late December that year it would undershoot analysts' estimates, sending the stock down $10.625, or 36%, to $19 in one day.

Ned Hazen, Avid's senior vice president of business development and corporate treasurer, said the firm last year decided it would kick the late-quarter discounting habit. It began to shift from direct sales to distributing more through resellers, adopted standardized discounts and reduced or eliminated end-of-quarter discounts and promotions. It took several quarters to convince customers it was serious he said. "There's a high degree of cynicism among customers: 'Yeah I hear you saying it, but let's see how you react at the 13th week of the quarter.'"

While Avid did fail to meet some of its revenue targets as it put its new policies in place, the impact on the already-languishing stock price was minimal. But thanks in part to reduced discounts, Avid was able to boost margins this year, beat first- and second-quarter estimates and see its stock soar to $34 from below $10 earlier this year.

Still, Gartner Group's Mr. Seay says it is rare for any company to continuously resist the pressure for discounts, because customers have become so skilled at extracting them.

And the arm-twisting has spread beyond discounts. Pilgrim Baxter's Mr. Smith says on occasion a company being acquired by another suddenly delays closing the deal near the end of the quarter. It then holds out for better terms, knowing the acquirer is expected to meet estimates based on the combined companies' earnings, he says.

Analysts have learned to spot the symptoms of a company dangerously addicted to discounting. "More backloading, more discounting, increases in accounts receivable, days outstanding, finally the company reaches the breaking point and it has to disappoint," says Mr. Rossi at Robertson Stephens.

One analyst says he has tried to spot hard-disk-drive makers in the act by calling up distributors late in the quarter, posing as a customer, to see "if they would make sure not to let a sale get away on the phone. Sometimes, I'd find prices would drop sharply over a one-week period. You'd say, 'What if I bought 10?" Suddenly you'd get a sweet price – a 20% drop."

The Wall Street Journal
September 16, 1997
Page C1

QUESTIONS FOR CONSIDERATION:

1. What does this article suggest to you about the importance of a company being able to generate accurate and timely financial information? What effects would you expect to see if a company developed a reputation for providing inaccurate financial information from its accounting department?

2. Why might "growth companies" be more susceptible to the types of pressures described in the article than other firms?

Name: ______________________ Professor: ______________________

Course: ______________________ Section: ______________________

Assignment 9
CURRENT ASSETS AND CURRENT LIABILITIES

Name of your company: ______________________

This assignment focuses on the current asset and current liability sections of the balance sheet and the related notes to the financial statements. Upon completion, you should understand your company's holdings of current assets and current liabilities and how effectively your company is managing them.

COMPLETING THE ASSIGNMENT:

1. Identify the changes in current asset and current liability accounts that occurred during the most recent accounting period.

	Amount on Most Recent Balance Sheet	Amount at End of Prior Year	Net Change in dollars	Net Change in percent
Current Assets:				
Cash & cash equivalents	______	______	______	____
Temporary investments [or short-term investments, or short-term marketable securities]	______	______	______	____
Accounts receivable, net	______	______	______	____
Other receivables, net	______	______	______	____
Inventories	______	______	______	____
Deferred (or prepaid) taxes	______	______	______	____
(other:) ______	______	______	______	____
Total current assets	______ *	______ *	______	____

*These two numbers should match the numbers on the balance sheet.

	Amount on Most Recent Balance Sheet	Amount at End of Prior Year	Net Change in Dollars	Net Change in Percent
Current Liabilities:				
Accounts payable	________	________	________	____
Short-term debt	________	________	________	____
Accrued salaries and wages	________	________	________	____
Accrued income taxes	________	________	________	____
Accrued interest	________	________	________	____
Current maturities of long-term debt	________	________	________	____
(other:) ________________	________	________	________	____
(other:) ________________	________	________	________	____
(other:) ________________	________	________	________	____
Total current liabilities	________ *	________ *	________	____

*These two numbers should match the numbers on the balance sheet.

2. What significant changes (in amount or percentage) occurred during the most recent year among the current assets and current liabilities? Are any of the changes troubling? Are there any that you might want to investigate further if you were an owner or creditor of your firm? Discuss.

____

____

____

____

____

____

____

____

____

____

3. Effective management of receivables is critical for most firms. Generally, the change in receivables should be consistent with the change in sales. Provide the following detailed information regarding sales, accounts receivable, and allowance for bad debts (also known as "allowance for uncollectible accounts). Hint: Some of this detail may be listed in the notes to the financial statements.

	End of Most Recent Year	End of Previous Year	Percent Change
a. Sales revenue	________	________	______
b. Gross accounts receivable	________	________	______
c. Less: Allowance for bad debts	________	________	______
d. Net accounts receivable	________	________	______
e. Allowance for bad debts as a percentage of sales	________	________	
f. Allowance for bad debts as a percentage of ending accounts receivable	________	________	

g. Are the percentage changes in accounts receivable and allowance for bad debts similar to the change in sales or are they different? Analyze and discuss the meaning or implications of any differences you observe.

____

____

____

____

____

____

____

____

____

____

____

4. Effective management of inventory is also critical for most firms. Changes in the levels of inventory should be consistent with changes in the level of cost of goods sold. For example, if the inventory balance increases sharply without a corresponding change in cost of goods sold, it may signal poor inventory management practices or sales expectations that did not materialize. Provide the following detailed information regarding cost of goods sold and the various categories of inventory. Hint: Some of this detail may be listed in the notes to the financial statements.

> **Note:** Not all firms have inventories. Companies that provide services instead of goods will not have meaningful amounts of inventory. For example, banks, insurance companies, electric power companies and airlines generally do not have meaningful amounts of inventory. As the United States moves to a more service-based economy there are more and more companies such as Federal Express (package delivery services) and H&R Block (income tax preparation services) that do not have inventory.
>
> If your firm is primarily a service firm without significant amounts of inventory you may skip this section. Ask your professor if he/she wishes you to substitute another firm's data for this section of the assignment.

	ACCOUNT BALANCES		
Item	End of Most Recent Year	End of Previous Year	Percent Change
a. Cost of goods sold	________	________	________
b. Merchandise inventory	________	________	________
c. Raw materials inventory	________	________	________
d. Work in process inventory	________	________	________
e. Finished goods inventory	________	________	________
f. (Other:) ____________	________	________	________
Total inventories held for resale	________ *	________ *	________

*sum of b, c, d, e, and f

g. Is the change in total inventories (and the change in each component of inventory) similar to the change in cost of goods sold or different? Discuss the implications of any differences you observe.

____

____

____

____

____

____

____

____

____

____

5. Which inventory valuation methods are used by your firm? (Mark all that apply.) Hint: This information usually is provided in the first note to the financial statements. Service firms probably won't have inventories.

> **Learning Note:** The Dollar-value LIFO, Retail LIFO, and Retail dollar-value LIFO methods listed below are merely specialized applications of the basic LIFO method you have learned about in class. In addition, almost every firm will report that they apply the lower-of-cost-or-market method. This means that the LIFO or FIFO amount does not exceed the cost of replacing the inventory (as used here, "market" means replacement cost).

i. Weighted-average _____

ii. FIFO _____

iii. LIFO _____

iv. Dollar-value LIFO _____

v. Retail LIFO _____

vi. Retail dollar-value LIFO _____

If more than one method is used, does one method predominate? If so, indicate that method below.

____

vii. Are inventories reported using lower-of-cost-or-market? _____

Learning Note: The following four ratios are computed to provide information about how well a firm manages its current assets and current liabilities. The computational formula and information content of each ratio is explained below.

a. **Current ratio (also known as the working capital ratio):** *current assets/current liabilities.* Shows how many dollars of current assets are available to pay off each dollar of current liabilities (as of the balance sheet date). This ratio measures liquidity: the ability of a company to pay its bills as they come due.

b. **Quick ratio (also known as the acid-test ratio):** *(cash + cash equivalents + short-term investments + accounts receivable) / current liabilities.* A "tighter" measure of liquidity in that inventory and prepaid expenses are excluded from the numerator.

c. **Accounts receivable turnover:** *sales revenue/average accounts receivable.* Measures the velocity of receivables through the firm. In general, the faster that receivables are collected the better. The higher the turnover the better.

d. **Inventory turnover:** *cost of goods sold/average inventory.* Yields an indicator of how long inventory is held before being sold. A high turnover is favorable and means that inventory is held only a short time before sale.

6. Calculate each of the following ratios for the most recent year available. Enter your results into the first column of the table below. For perspective, compare your firm's ratios for the most recent year to those of your classmates' firms.

	Your	CLASSMATES' FIRMS				
	Firm	**Firm 1**	**Firm 2**	**Firm 3**	**Firm 4**	**Firm 5**
a. Current ratio	_____	_____	_____	_____	_____	_____
b. Quick ratio (Acid-test ratio)	_____	_____	_____	_____	_____	_____
c. Accounts receivable turnover	_____	_____	_____	_____	_____	_____
d. Inventory turnover	_____	_____	_____	_____	_____	_____

7. How do your firm's ratios compare to those of your classmates' firms? Are they high, low, about the same? Is there anything specific about your firm, its industry, or your classmates' firms or industries that might tend to explain the differences between your company's ratios and those of the other firms? Discuss.

Reading 9-A

Microsoft's Problem Is What Many Firms Just Wish They Had

The Biggest Software Maker Accumulates Cash Faster Than It Can Spend It

By DAVID BANK
Staff Reporter of The Wall Street Journal

Microsoft Corp. faces a quandary that many companies would like to share: It is accumulating cash far faster than it can spend it.

When the world's largest software company discloses financial results today for the fiscal second quarter ended Dec. 31, it will probably report cash holdings and short-term investments of about $9 billion, almost double the amount at mid-1995. The figure includes about $980 million from last month's issue of convertible preferred stock but nonetheless indicates that Microsoft's corc operations are generating huge stockpiles of cash and at a rate about double that of two years ago.

But, as Midas found, Microsoft's golden touch brings its own difficulties, With cash now representing about 70% of Microsoft's total assets, analysts say the low yield on the cash holdings could become a drag on its overall performance and eventually on the highflying price of its stock. The cash is held in short-term investments and Treasury securities that yielded an annual rate of about 5.8% in the fiscal first quarter.

For now, with Microsoft's earnings strong, shareholders are hardly screaming for action, but that could change if performance lags. Institutional investors are not paying these valuations for Microsoft to put the money in municipal bonds," says David Readerman, an analyst at "Montgomery Securities in San Francisco.

Microsoft's predicament is unlike that of any other company with tons of cash. For one thing, it has very little manufacturing expense to sop up liquidity, with gross margins hovering near an outlandish 90%. By contrast, Intel Corp.'s cash is growing at even a faster rate, leaping $2.1 billion in the fourth quarter alone to $8.2 billion, but the chip giant has to invest enormous sums in new plants and plans to increase its capital spending $1.5 billion this year.

Moreover, the Justice Department is unlikely to allow Microsoft to acquire major companies within the software industry, and Microsoft is unlikely to find acquisitions outside the industry that will provide it with a rate of return anywhere near its 32% return on equity. For tax and other reasons, shareholders of any company acquired by Microsoft are apt to prefer stock rather than cash.

Nonetheless, the company's filings state that the cash is managed so as to be quickly available for a large-scale acquisition if the opportunity arises, and there is reason to believe Microsoft is willing to invest in publishing and entertainment concerns for strategic reasons. One of Microsoft's central objectives is to turn its operating systems into platforms for receiving multimedia offerings. Before Turner Broadcasting Systems merged with Time Warner Inc., Microsoft Chairman Bill Gates was reportedly in negotiations to invest $2 billion in Turner's Cable Network News.

"There's huge leverage in content," said J. William Gurley, an analyst with Deutsche Morgan Grenfell Inc. in Palo Alto, Calif.

Strategic Value Is Key

Microsoft clearly is interested only in acquisitions that fill a strategic need. Most mistakes in the acquisition arena are made by companies blundering into unrelated businesses.

"We want to manage high rates of return, but on the other hand, the long term goal of our cash is to utilize it for our business," said Greg Maffei, Microsoft's treasurer. "We look to make investments where we think it's a good strategic value as well as a good equity investment."

Since the Justice Department's successful blockage of Microsoft's attempt to acquire Intuit Inc. in 1994 for $2.3 billion of stock, the company has focused on small deals. During the past three years the company has spent $1.5 billion in 47 acquisitions, joint ventures and minority-equity investments. But any major increase in acquisition activity risks flooding the market with investment capital, Microsoft's cash hoard is about equal to the total of all the venture-capital pools available for technology investments.

The modest spending spree hasn't seriously affected the cash reserves because most of the deals have been for stock. "Unfortunately, we have this terrible thing that people want our stock," said Mr. Maffei. "We would prefer to pay cash." Mr. Maffei understands the logic of the sellers. "The choice for them is: Do I want to get after-tax dollars, or do I want to have Bill Gates manage my money on a pretax basis?"

Another option for draining cash is to pay a dividend to shareholders. Indeed, Microsoft's recent issue of convertible preferred shares was advertised as a way to allow investors interested in dividend payments to participate in Microsoft's prosperity. That stock pays a dividend of 2.75% and also allows the holders to receive a maximum of 28% of any capital appreciation of Microsoft's common shares over a three-year period.

But analysts say there is little likelihood that Microsoft will issue a dividend on its common stock for the simple reason that the main recipient of such a payout, Mr. Gates, one of the country's richest men, has no need for the money and even less need for the taxes he would incur. In addition, Mr. Gates, holder of nearly 24% of the company's stock, appears to believe that dividends are inappropriate for a fast-growing technology concern with many opportunities.

Stock Repurchases

The convertible preferred offering was billed as a way to offer dividends to conservative investors. Its main purpose, however, appears to be to offset the rising cost of stock buybacks used to fulfill employees' stock options. The company's gross buybacks increased to $1.3 billion in fiscal 1996, ended June 30, from $348 million in 1994. The preferred, because it only allows holders as much as 28% of the common stock's appreciation, gives Microsoft the right to buy back about 12 million converted shares in three years at a maximum price of $102.24 a share. That price could be one-third to one-half of the then current market price if Microsoft's stock appreciates at its historical rate.

Of course, reducing the buyback costs by such an amount will only help increase the cash hoard. And under the right circumstances, Microsoft could issue a similar preferred issue regularly.

"It's entirely conceivable that Microsoft will do this again if certain variables such as cash position, share price and management's view of operating prospects come into alignment," says Jonathan Cohen, a Smith Barney Inc. analyst.

Yesterday, in trading on the Nasdaq Stock Market, Microsoft closed at $86, up $1.375, or 1.6%. Its 52-week high is $86.375.

The Wall Street Journal
January 17, 1997
Page A3

Questions For Consideration:

1. What facts in the article imply that Microsoft's financial situation is different than that of most companies?

2. Why do you think Microsoft is in this position?

Reading 9-B

Around the World in 180 Days

If you're not careful, that's how long it could take you to collect international receivables

By JILL ANDRESKY FRASER

Congratulations! Your company's plan for global diversification is a wild success, with sales orders rolling in from absolutely everywhere. Or should we offer our condolences? Now you've got to figure out how to collect all those international accounts receivable.

Unfortunately, the realities of foreign collections can be downright shocking. "Take a country like Malaysia," says Stephen Chipman, the director of international services for accounting firm Grant Thornton's southwestern U.S. division, based in Dallas. "If you say COD, Malaysian companies interpret that as meaning payment is due in 30 days. Then you're lucky if they get around to paying you within 90 days."

Les Kirschbaum, president of Mid-Continent Agencies, an international collection company in Rolling Meadows, Ill., agrees about the difficulties of collecting foreign receivables. "U.S. companies make a big mistake when they assume that they can deal with problem foreign accounts the same way they do here, just by hiring an attorney or a collection agency. No way," says Kirschbaum. "In countries like Mexico, for example, the legal process involved with chasing after a problem payer is very, very complicated."

Because problems with foreign receivables are easier to avoid in advance than to clear up afterward, here's a guide to help both novice and full-fledged exporters navigate their way around foreign collection hazards.

Stage One: "We're negotiating an overseas sale. What should I do before signing on the dotted line?"

Before figuring out how to price your sale and design its terms, you need to learn as much as you can about the country's payment norms, creditor protection laws (if any), and your customer's credit history. To quantify the risks, start by checking with your regional branch of the Export-Import Bank, as well as the U.S. Chamber of Commerce.

"Even if you've sold goods or services to a foreign company in the past, it makes sense to check up regularly on changes in its country's economic or political risks," says Kirschbaum. "We always warn companies that if they extend credit, they're extending it to a country as well as a company."

Then check out your potential customer as carefully as you would a new domestic client. Good sources of information are your accounting firm (if it has international offices or connections to an international network), your international bank, and most credit-reporting services.

Tip for novices: Until you learn to finesse the complexities of foreign markets, take a conservative stance. At the very least, that means walking away from any sale that would have scared you off on the domestic scene.

Stage Two: "After doing some research, I still want to make the sale. What terms make the best sense?"

Start by insisting on payment up front. If your customer agrees, life as an exporter will be a whole lot simpler. "We're pretty blunt about telling new customers that until we get to know them better, we insist on payment in advance — for which we give them a 2% price discount — or payment through a confirmed, irrevocable letter of credit," says John Kirchgeorg, the owner of Life Corp., a manufacturer of emergency oxygen units in Milwaukee. "We won't loosen terms until a client has proved that it's worthy of our trust. Otherwise, it's too risky."

What if a foreign customer goes for the letter-of-credit option? Don't automatically accept, advises Grant Thornton's Chipman. "You've got to check out the creditworthiness of your customer's bank to make certain it will be willing and able to release payment as the customer receives your goods or services." The best way to check out a foreign bank is with the assistance of your own local bank. If it can't help, try the U.S. Chamber of Commerce.

Tip for novices: If you're afraid of losing business because your terms are too strict, consider insuring your foreign receivables. (It will cost you, but not as much as a deadbeat customer will.) The Export Import Bank offers a variety of insurance packages, including some aimed at small businesses and short-term buyers of single policies.

Stage Three: We've agreed on the payment terms. Now my worries are behind me, right?"

Sad to say, exporters need to protect themselves against *currency* risks as well as credit risks — even when their customers are in countries that seem safe. "I remember back in 1992 when the British and French currencies took a nose dive. A lot of exporters were shocked to learn that they could lose 25% of the value of their receivables overnight," recalls Chipman. "Don't delude yourself into thinking you're at risk only in a volatile Eastern European or third world country."

When you're dealing with large accounts or extending sales terms over an indefinite period, consider a strategy relied on by most large corporations: currency hedging, which allows companies that expect to receive their payments in foreign currency to lock in a predictable conversion rate. But the downside is that buying the hedge can be pricey. Another alternative: set up a foreign bank account closer to your customers, which can result in quicker collections and minimize currency risks.

Tip for novices: Keep things simple (and inexpensive) by insisting on payment in U.S. dollars. If your potential customer won't agree, move on.

Inc.
April 1997
Page 106-107

QUESTION FOR CONSIDERATION:

1. Identify three different sources of difficulty that can cause a company problems when selling goods internationally on credit.

2. If collection of international receivables is such a problem, why would a rational business person bother trying to make international sales?

Name: ______________________ Professor: ______________

Course: ______________________ Section: ______________

Assignment 10
LONG-TERM ASSETS

Name of your company ______________________________

In this assignment you will review and evaluate the decisions your company's management has made regarding long-lived assets. This includes plant (or fixed) assets, intangible assets, and long-term investments.

COMPLETING THE ASSIGNMENT:

1. Identify the changes in your firm's long-term asset accounts that occurred during the most recent accounting period. You will probably have to search the footnotes to obtain some of the specific account information requested. Blank spaces have been provided for you to write in any additional items that appear in your company's Annual Report or SEC 10-K under long-term assets.

	Amount on Most Recent Balance Sheet	Amount at End of Prior Year	Net Change in Dollars	Net Change in Percent
Long-term Assets:				
Machinery and equipment	______	______	______	____
Buildings (and leasehold improvements)	______	______	______	____
Land	______	______	______	____
(other) ____________	______	______	______	____
(other) ____________	______	______	______	____
(other) ____________	______	______	______	____
Less: Accumulated dep.	______	______	______	____
Net* plant, property and equipment	______	______	______	____

*Original cost of depreciable assets minus accumulated depreciation to date.

Long-term Assets: (continued from prior page)

	Amount on Most Recent Balance Sheet	Amount at End of Prior Year	Net Change in Dollars	Net Change in Percent
Construction in progress	______	______	______	____
Deferred (or prepaid) taxes	______	______	______	____
Long-term receivables	______	______	______	____
Long-term investments	______	______	______	____
Excess of cost over net assets of acquired companies (i.e., goodwill)	______	______	______	____
Patents, copyrights, and trademarks	______	______	______	____
(other) ______________	______	______	______	____
(other) ______________	______	______	______	____
Total long-term assets	______*	______*	______	____

*These amounts should match the totals on the balance sheet.

2. Based on the information above, briefly summarize the significant changes in long-term asset accounts, if any, that occurred during the most recent year.

____

____

____

____

____

____

____

____

____

____

____

____

____

____

3. Accounting policies related to long-term assets: (Hint: Most of this information will be found in the first note to the financial statements.)

> **Learning Note:** The terms depreciation, amortization, and depletion are used to indicate very similar processes. All refer to the process of allocating part of the cost of a long-term asset to expense. When allocating a portion of the cost of tangible fixed assets to expense, accountants use the term "depreciation". When referring to this process for intangible assets, accountants use the term "amortization". When referring to this process for natural resource assets, accountants use the term "depletion."

a. Depreciation: Which depreciation method(s) does the firm use for financial reporting purposes? Check all that apply.

i. Straight-line _____

ii. Sum-of-the-year's digits _____

iii. Declining-balancc _____

iv. Other (specify) _______________

v. If multiple depreciation methods are used, which method is used predominantly?

____

vi. Does your firm disclose the estimated useful lives that it assumes for depreciating its tangible fixed assets. If yes, describe them.

____

____

____

b. Does your firm report any intangible assets on the balance sheet? If yes, describe the policies (e.g., method and estimated life) your firm uses to compute amortization expense.

____

____

____

____

c. Does your firm report any natural resource assets? If yes, describe the policies (e.g., method and estimated useful life) your firm uses to compute depletion expense.

____

____

____

____

> **Learning Note:** When one firm controls another firm (such as by owning more than 50% of its voting stock), the second firm is a subsidiary of the first and consolidated financial statements are presented. Consolidated statements combine the financial information of the subsidiaries with that of the parent firm. Use of the term "consolidated" in the title of financial statements indicates that the firm controls at least one other firm.

4. Does your firm own one or more subsidiaries? Hint: Does your firm present "Consolidated" financial statements (e.g., consolidated balance sheet, consolidated income statement)?

   a. Yes ____ No ____

   b. If the answer to part a. above was yes, determine whether all the subsidiaries are 100% wholly-owned. Hint: If any subsidiary is only partially owned, there will be an account listed on the balance sheet (usually after long-term liabilities but before stockholders' equity) with a title *something like* "Minority Interest." Check one of the following.

      i. All subsidiaries are 100% wholly-owned. ____

      ii. At least one subsidiary is less than 100% wholly-owned. ____

> **Learning Note:** In general, when a company owns stock of another firm, but not enough to control the firm, this ownership of shares is accounted for as an "Investment" and is reported under long-term assets on the investor company's balance sheet.

c. Did your firm report any investments in other firms on its balance sheet under the category of long-term investments?

Yes ____ No ____

d. If yes, inspect the notes to the financial statements to determine which of the following accounting methods are used by your firm to account for this investment(s). Mark all of the following that apply.

i. Cost method _____
ii. Mark-to-market (or fair value) method _____
iii. Equity method _____

e. Did your firm acquire or dispose of any subsidiaries or investments in other firms during the most recent year? Hint: This will be discussed in the notes if it occurred. It will probably also show up on the statement of cash flows.

Yes ____ No ____

f. If yes, describe the acquisitions or disposals that occurred.

____

____

____

____

____

____

____

____

____

____

____

Learning Note: The following four ratios yield information about a company's use of long-term assets. The computational formula and the information content of each ratio is explained below.

a. **Depreciation and amortization to average long-term assets:** *(depreciation expense + amortization expense)/ average* long-term assets.* This ratio yields an indication of how rapidly the firm is expensing (writing off) its long-term assets. This can be critical in an industry experiencing rapidly changing technology.

b. **Long-term assets to total assets:** *long-term assets/ total assets.* This ratio yields information about a firm's financial flexibility. The larger the portion of long-term assets, the less flexibility the firm has to change strategies quickly.

c. **Plant assets to total assets:** *plant assets/ total assets.* This ratio also yields information about financial flexibility but focuses only on the investment in land, buildings, and equipment, etc.

d. **Sales to average plant assets:** *sales/ average plant assets.* This ratio measures productivity of the plant assets. It shows how many dollars of sales were generated by each dollar invested in plant assets. How hard are the plant assets working?

*(current year's ending balance + prior year's ending balance)/2

5. Compute each of the four ratios above for the most recent year and enter the result in the first column below. To give perspective to your results, check with five classmates to determine the value of the ratios for their firms. Record the information below.

Ratio	Your Firm	CLASSMATES' FIRMS Firm 1	Firm 2	Firm 3	Firm 4	Firm 5
i. dep + amort / ave. L-term assets	______	______	______	______	______	______
ii. Long-term assets / total assets	______	______	______	______	______	______
iii. plant assets / total assets	______	______	______	______	______	______
iv. sales / ave. plant assets	______	______	______	______	______	______

e. How do your firm's long-term asset ratios compare to those of your classmates' firms? Are they high, low, about the same? Is there anything specific about your firm, its industry, or your classmates' firms or industries that tend to explain the differences between your company's long-term asset ratios and those of the other firms? Discuss and explain.

Reading 10

Searching for Nonfiction in Financial Statements

The Glamorous World Of Accounting Standards

By Justin Fox

Spend some time watching the members of the Financial Accounting Standards Board in action, and it's hard not to think of them as heroes. Seriously. Beset by conniving earnings-manipulating corporations, betrayed by spineless Big Six accounting firms, these seven brave Defenders of Our Nation's Accounting Principles do battle on behalf of investors who need the numbers on financial reports to mean something. At least, that's how it looks from close up, especially during the board's recent bitter struggle to make corporations report the cost of the stock options they give out.

The FASB's valiant efforts over the years may, however, have been largely an exercise in missing the point. Financial statements — in particular the earnings numbers they produce — have actually become less reliable as a measure of corporate performance and value. One study on the topic, by New York University accounting professor Baruch Lev, documents a sharp drop during the past few decades in the statistical correlation between reported earnings and stock returns. This may simply mean investors have gone nuts, but Lev offers other explanations. The most compelling: The Generally Accepted Accounting Principles, set by FASB, don't allow for some of the prime drivers of corporate success — investments in intangible assets such as know-how, patents, brands, and customer loyalty.

The great strength of modern accounting is that it leads managers and investors to draw links between a company's wealth (assets) and the income it derives from that wealth — thus focusing their attention on return on investment and leading them to attempt to maximize that return. Accounting also links spending and revenue over time, so the cost of building a plant that will produce earnings for 20 years is counted as an asset and charged to earnings over 20 years, not all at once. Leaving the most important assets off the balance sheet, and counting money spent on them as immediate expenses, gives readers of financial reports — including company executives — a distorted picture of how a company makes money.

No one disputes that current accounting practice misrepresents reality. "There are arguments that balance sheets ignore certain intangibles," acknowledges former FASB chairman Donald Kirk. "But the reporting issues of trying to recognize them are, in my mind, insurmountable." The concern of many accountants is that companies will try to classify virtually every expenditure as an asset in an attempt to jack up book value and defer expenses. Financial analysts express similar worries — and point to America Online, which, until backing down in October, capitalized most of the costs of recruiting new subscribers as assets, even though it couldn't claim with any confidence that those customers would stick around. But successful established companies often do just the opposite. Microsoft, for example, despite its massive investment in know-how, claims no significant intangible assets. A special FASB rule tells software companies to capitalize some R&D spending, but Microsoft says intangibles are just too hard to keep track of. The company's no-intangibles accounting policy also happens to make its earnings growth look even more impressive, and gives it a truly spectacular return-on-assets number.

Between AOL's overreaching and Microsoft's hauteur, however, are (as has been documented in this magazine) more and more companies whose executives realize that to manage their resources properly, they need to keep track of intangible assets and the returns on those assets. Securities and Exchange Commissioner Steven Wallman is convinced that some of these measures, such as R&D spending and customer satisfaction indexes, are becoming reliable enough to be included as supplements to companies' annual reports. "Not only am I confident that there is a way to do it right," Wallman says, "I'm overwhelmingly confident that we have to do it, because right now we know that the answers we've got are wrong." Lev, who in October founded the Intangibles Research Center at NYU, believes that measurements of R&D spending are already reliable enough to be included as an asset on the balance sheet.

All these measures are, of course, inexact. But so are many of the numbers one now finds on corporate balance sheets. To argue that intangibles don't belong in financial reports is to argue that it's more important for those reports to follow accounting tradition than to reflect economic reality. Which is fine for the professional analysts, whose trade group offers a course on Finding Reality in Reported Earnings. But for the rest of us, as long as companies reporting intangible assets have to follow some consistent rules, what's wrong with earnings numbers that actually bear a resemblance to reality?

Fortune
December 23, 1996
Pages 38 - 40

QUESTIONS FOR CONSIDERATION:

1. The article claims that Microsoft's accounting policy regarding intangibles "...makes its earnings growth look even more impressive, and gives it a truly spectacular return-on-assets number." Carefully explain how the policy has the claimed effect on earnings and how it has the claimed effect on return-on-assets.

2. What is the primary argument against reporting intangibles such as know-how, internally developed patents or brands, or customer loyalty as assets? Do you agree with this point of view? Why or why not?

Name: ______________________ Professor: ______________

Course: ______________________ Section: ______________

Assignment 11
LONG-TERM LIABILITIES

Name of your company: ______________________

The purpose of this assignment is to understand and evaluate the decisions your company's management has made regarding long-term liabilities.

KEY REFERENCES FOR THIS ASSIGNMENT:

a. *Moody's Bond Record*, Moody's Investors Service (a monthly service), or

b. *Standard and Poor's Bond Guide*, Standard & Poor's, Inc. (a monthly service)

COMPLETING THE ASSIGNMENT:

1. Identify the changes in the long-term liability accounts that occurred during the most recent accounting period. Blank spaces have been provided for you to write in additional items that appear in your firm's long-term liability section.

	Amount on Most Recent Balance Sheet	Amount at End of Prior Year	Net Change in Dollars	Net Change in Percent
Long-term Liabilities:				
Long-term debt	______	______	______	____
Capitalized lease obligations	______	______	______	____
Deferred income taxes	______	______	______	____
Pension liability	______	______	______	____
(other:) ____________	______	______	______	____
(other:) ____________	______	______	______	____
Total long-term liabilities	______	______	______	____

2. Based on the information on the previous page and that found in the notes to the financial statements, briefly summarize the significant changes, if any, in the long-term liability accounts during the most recent year.

____

____

____

____

____

____

____

____

____

____

____

____

____

____

3. What are the approximate interest rates incurred on your firm's long-term liabilities? Complete the schedule below. Some items (e.g., deferred income taxes) do not incur interest. Some (or most) of this information will be found in the notes to the financial statements.

Long-term Liability accounts:	Approximate Rate of Interest
______________________	________%
______________________	________%
______________________	________%
______________________	________%
______________________	________%
______________________	________%

4. What amount of cash is the firm obligated to pay out in each of the next five years for repayment of long-term debt, capitalized lease obligations, operating leases, and/or other commitments? (This information usually is contained in the notes to the financial statements and will take careful reading to identify.)

Year	**Repayment of long-term debt**	**Capital lease obligations**	**Operating leases**	**Other commitments**
Year 1	________	________	________	________
Year 2	________	________	________	________
Year 3	________	________	________	________
Year 4	________	________	________	________
Year 5	________	________	________	________
Totals	________	________	________	________

Go to the statement of cash flows. Observe the amount of "net cash flow from operations" generated in each of the last three years. To what extent does it appear that the company will be able to pay off the above scheduled obligations each year with cash generated from operations? Might the company need to raise the required cash in some other way? Discuss.

____

____

____

____

____

____

____

5. Find and read the note (to the financial statements) about your firm's pension plan(s). Then, answer the following questions.

   a. Which type(s) of pension plan does your firm have? Check all that apply. The firm may have either type of plan, both, or none.

      Defined contribution plan ____ Defined benefit plan ____ None ____

b. What is the relationship between the pension obligations your firm's employees have earned and the assets of your firm's pension plan? Fill in the blanks for the information items (i.) through (vi.) below.

i. Fair value of pension plan assets ________________

ii. Less: accumulated benefit obligation (ABO) ________________

iii. Excess (deficiency) of plan assets over ABO ________________

> **Learning Note:** The accumulated benefit obligation (ABO) is the present value of all pension benefits that employees have earned to date based on their current wage rates.

iv. Fair value of pension plan assets ________________

v. Less: projected benefit obligation (PBO) ________________

vi. Excess (deficiency) of plan assets over PBO ________________

> **Learning Note:** The projected benefit obligation (PBO) is the present value of all pension benefits that employees have earned to date based on their expected wage rates at the time they retire.

d. If the company were liquidated today, would there be enough pension plan assets for the firm to meet its obligations to its employees? Explain. (Hint: focus on the ABO.)

____

____

____

____

e. If you acquired the company and its employees today, are there be enough pension plan assets to cover benefits earned-to-date when the employees retire at their normal retirement dates? Explain. (Hint: focus on the PBO.)

____

____

____

____

6. Identify the investment characteristics of your firm's long-term debt. Obtain the most recent monthly issue of either Moody's Bond Record or Standard & Poor's Bond Guide. (If you have a choice, Moody's Bond Record is a little easier to use.) Look up your company to determine whether it has any long-term debt listed. (Companies are listed alphabetically in both publications.) Answer each of the following questions for each issue of long-term debt. (If your firm has more than three issues, select three representative issues for listing here.)

	Long-Term Debt Issue #1	**Long-Term Debt Issue #2**	**Long-Term Debt Issue #3**
a. Type of debt (notes, subordinated notes, senior notes, debentures, etc.)	____________	____________	____________
b. Interest rate	____________	____________	____________
c. Year debt is due	____________	____________	____________
d. Debt rating (indicate which rating source you used):			
____ Moody's	____________	____________	____________
____ S&P	____________	____________	____________
e. Indicate whether the issue is "investment grade" (rated Baa/BBB or higher) or "speculative grade" (i.e. "junk bonds"). If your company has no bonds rated by Moody's or S&P, leave the rest of this page blank.			
	____________	____________	____________
f. Call date of the debt (if any)	____________	____________	____________
g. Call price of the debt (if any)	____________	____________	____________
h. Current market price	____________	____________	____________
i. Recent price range: highest price	____________	____________	____________
lowest price	____________	____________	____________
j. Yield to maturity	____________	____________	____________

7. Did your firm disclose any contingencies, sometimes called contingent liabilities, in the notes to the financial statements? Discuss the specific nature of these contingencies and how (or whether) they are expected to affect the firm's financial health.

Learning Note: The following two ratios are computed to provide information about how a company is managing its long-term liabilities. The computational formula and information content of each ratio is explained below.

a. **Debt to total assets ratio:** *total liabilities/total assets.* This ratio reveals the percentage of assets financed by debt. The use of debt financing is referred to as financial leverage. The higher the degree of financial leverage, the higher the risk that a company will not be able to meet its interest payments and will be forced into bankruptcy.

b. **Times interest earned**: *[net income + (interest expense (1 - tax rate))] ÷ interest expense.* This ratio measures the cushion a company has regarding its ability to pay interest charges on its debt. The higher the cushion, the more likely the company is to be able to meet its interest payments.

8. Calculate each of the following ratios for the most recent year. Use the computational formulas shown in the Learning Note at the bottom of the previous page that are reproduced below.

a. Debt to total assets = $\frac{\text{total liabilities}}{\text{total assets}}$

Debt to total assets = -- = ________%

b. Times interest earned* = $\frac{\text{net income + [interest expense (1 - tax rate)]}}{\text{interest expense}}$

Times interest earned = ------------------------------------ = ________

*Many companies report a number on the income statement using the title *operating income*. This amount is often used in the numerator of this ratio instead of the more complex computation shown above. If your company reports *operating income*, use it in the numerator of this ratio.

9. Enter your results into the first column of the table below. For perspective, compare your firm's ratios for the most recent year to those of your classmates' firms.

Ratio	Your Firm	CLASSMATES' FIRMS Firm 1	Firm 2	Firm 3	Firm 4	Firm 5
i. Debt to total assets ratio	______	______	______	______	______	______
ii. Times interest earned	______	______	______	______	______	______

10. How do your firm's ratios compare to those of your classmates' firms? Are they high, low, about the same? Is there anything specific about your firm, its industry, or your classmates' firms or industries that might tend to explain the differences between your company's ratios and those of the other firms? Discuss, using the space here and on the next page.

____

____

____

____

Reading 11-A

Corporate Treasurers Rush to Sell Bonds

Low Interest Rates, Strong Economy Spur Borrowing

By R. BLEAKLEY
Staff Reporter of The Wall Street Journal

Like dozens of other companies recently, Aramark Corp. saw the bargain sign flashing on Wall Street.

So, after waiting more than a year to tap the public bond market, the Philadelphia managed-services firm made its move Thursday, raising $125 million at an attractive annual rate of 7.10% over 10 years. As interest rates have fallen, corporations have raised more than $30 billion in the past seven weeks, a sign of confidence that business will remain strong in 1997.

"This brightens the economic outlook," said John Lonski, chief economist of Moody's Investors Service Inc. "I'd be more worried about next year if corporations were avoiding the bond market because rates were too high."

"Opportunistic" issuers, the securities industry's term for bargain hunters that are not routinely seeking funds, have included in recent months Coca-Cola Enterprises Inc., Xerox Corp., Bristol-Myers Squibb Co., Anadarko Petroleum Corp., Rubbermaid Inc. and a host of high-yield telecommunications industry issuers such as Sprint Spectrum Inc.

Irresistible Opportunity

For Aramark, the chance to grab such a low rate for its bonds was "irresistible," said Barbara Austell, the company's treasurer. It wasn't just that interest rates had come down (the yield on the Treasury's benchmark 30-year bond had dropped below 6.5% from more than 7% in late September). But the margin above the Treasury bond rate that companies pay to attract bond investors had narrowed as well. As a result, Aramark's 7.10% rate for its 10-year bond issue was a marked improvement over the 8.15% the company is paying for a similar deal issued in May 1995. The difference saves about $1.3 million a year in pretax interest charges.

"When Treasury bonds got below the psychological threshold of 6.75%, corporate bond offerings picked up," noted Diane Vazza, head of fixed-income research at Standard & Poor's Corp. "Anything below 6.5% is a go."

Sears Roebuck Acceptance Corp., which recently issued $300 million of bonds to help fund its consumer-finance business, was spurred by the fact that 10-year Treasury bond issues were trading at levels rarely seen in the past 20 years. "That's one of the signals we look at," said Alice Peterson, treasurer of the parent company, Sears, Roebuck & Co. "So we said this is not a bad time to get a good chunk in one fell swoop."

High-Quality Issuers

Investment bankers say there are plenty of buyers for corporate bonds because bond mutual funds and insurance companies are flush with cash and the quality of the issuers has been strong. Even in the junk-bond market, which is on track to set a record in the amount of funds raised, there is a greater preponderance of higher-rated issues. "This is not the schlock of the 1980's" said Bennett Goodman, head of the high-yield department at Donaldson, Lufkin & Jenrette Securities. "We're seeing the likes of Advanced Micro Devices Inc., Teleport Communications Group and Sprint Spectrum, all fast-growing, young companies that are likely to be upgraded some day."

There has even been a market for 100-year bonds, only a handful of which have been issued in modern times. Earlier this month, Times Mirror Co. and Anadarko Petroleum issued bonds that will mature in the year 2096. For Anadarko, it was the second such offering of late. In September, the Houston-based independent driller raised $100 million in a deal priced to yield 7.73% a year that investors could "put," or sell, back to the company after 30 years if interest rates were higher at that time. The latest issue is even better. It pays investors only 7.25% a year and cannot be sold back to Anadarko until maturity a century later.

Xerox Pulls the Trigger

Xerox "took advantage of insurance company appetites," said assistant treasurer George Roth. It hadn't anticipated selling any of the $1.2 billion in debt securities registered in early October so quickly. "But when the market rallied big time and moved more and more in our directions we pulled the trigger" on a $350 million deal last Wednesday, he said.

Most companies like Xerox could have afforded to wait, because they have ready access to lower-priced variable-rate floating debt either from banks or in the commercial-paper market. By locking in an attractive fixed rate, however, they can remove the uncertainty of paying dearly if rates suddenly rise. They also leave themselves more flexibility to take on more short-term debt as opportunities occur.

Coca-Cola Enterprises, too, jumped at the chance this fall to turn part of its commercial paper outstanding into fixed rate long-term debt. Even though 1993 was the last time it had issued public market debt, it raised $600 million in two offerings in October and another $250 million in November. "As interest rates reached unpredicted lows, the debt markets have looked particularly attractive," said treasurer Vicki Roman.

Other companies are turning to the bond markets to finance expansions. Rubbermaid took its maiden voyage into the public bond market last Wednesday in a deal led by J.P. Morgan & Co. The offering raised $150 million to help pay for Rubbermaid's recent acquisition of Graco Inc., the toy company. Advanced Micro Devices will use the $400 million it raised in August for its new generation of high speed computer chips.

While the lower interest rates are a sign the economy is slowing, recent bond issuers are upbeat about their own prospects. "Our business is moving very well," said Bristol-Myers Squibb's chief financial officer, Michael Mee. The pharmaceutical giant raised $350 million in a 30-year bond offering Nov. 12., he said, because "we anticipate future development needs." As to whether rates might go lower, Mr. Mee said, "we have a shelf registration of $650 million. If we were wrong on this being the bottom of the rate cycle, we can go in for more."

As long as rates remain at least near present levels for a while, the slate of new offerings is likely to be large well into the first quarter of 1997. Moody's Mr. Ionski notes that shelf registrations of securities not yet sold is at its highest level in more than three years. "That implies corporations are far from completing their long term borrowing intentions," he said.

The Wall Street Journal
November 25, 1996
Page A2

Questions For Consideration:

1. If you have access to the Internet, visit the following web site address: *www.stocktrader.com/yc2.html.* Under the column labeled "CURVE," find the current yield (YLD) on 30-year Treasury bonds. At the time this article was written, the yield (or return) on the 30-year Treasury bond was approximately 6.5%. What is the yield today? Does today's yield suggest a more attractive bond market for corporate treasurers or a less attractive market? Why?

2. In October of 1997, Safra Republic Holdings SA (a company based in Luxembourg) issued $250 million of the world's first 1,000-year bonds. What similarities and differences do you see between *really* long-term bonds (either the 100-year variety or the 1,000-year variety) and nonredeemable preferred stock? Analyze them from the perspective of both the issuing company and the investor. Do you observe any *meaningful* differences? Discuss.

Reading 11-B

The Art of the Covenant

THOU SHALT NOT LET THY CURRENT LIABILITIES EXCEED THY CURRENT ASSETS

By Jill Andresky Fraser

Two years ago Allen Systems Group Inc., a computer-software manufacturer based in Naples, Fla., was almost ready to sign a new credit agreement. But its chief financial officer, Frederick Roberts, was concerned about an essential yet often-overlooked component of the deal: the loan covenants.

"Our banker wanted to include some very strict covenants regarding the company's key financial ratios," Roberts recalls. Those covenants "would have wound up hampering our ability to grow, because they would have prevented us from acquiring some important new software products. Each acquisition would have put us temporarily out of compliance."

Roberts was determined to negotiate the $23-million company's way out of those requirements — or seek financing elsewhere. "Too many entrepreneurs get ecstatic just over the act of qualifying for bank funding — but then fail to pay attention to the fine print of the loan agreement," he says. "If you're not watching and you fall out of compliance with a covenant, you run a very powerful risk of getting your loan called in, whether you're up-to-date on your payments or not."

Loan-covenant problems are fairly common for fast-growing companies, whose financial statements seldom conform to a banker's ideal vision of fiscal health. Roberts, armed with short- and long-term financial projections, eventually won "more appropriate" terms, as he puts it. But many other companies either don't try to change their bank covenants or don't worry about future problems those covenants might pose.

Would your own approach have been simply to sign up, close the loan, and hope for the best? Then it's time for *Inc.'s* quick primer on loan covenants. Don't visit your banker without it.

MYTH: With bank financing, all that matters is the interest rate.

REALITY: Many banking experts believe that interest charges are among the *least* important features of a loan. "After all, interest is a deductible business expense, so the government is really helping you handle it," notes George M. Dawson, a banking consultant based in San Antonio, Tex.

Loan covenants, on the other hand, are extremely important to your banker. A violation of a loan covenant is "the bank's early-warning system that something *might* be going on in your company that's a sign of trouble," Dawson explains. "It's like a blip suddenly appearing on the radar that tells the bank to pull its loan before

NOW WHAT? TAKE THIS TO THE BANK

It's not easy navigating your way through the loan-covenant jungle, especially at a time when bank mergers have added inches to many boilerplate documents. Here are five steps that should help:

1. Find out whether your prospective bank plans to retain your loan or sell it. In the latter case, there's probably less room for maneuvering over covenant issues.
2. Inquire about the bank's expertise in — and funding experience with — your industry. Covenants from industry specialists are often more realistic.
3. Ask to see a sample list of covenants before the date of the closing, so that you can avoid a situation in which desperation for funds—or a lack of careful analysis — persuade you to simply sign anything. Make certain that you can live with the bank's terms about the consequences of going out of compliance.
4. Do a computer run of your company's past performance during the most recent one-, two-, and three-year periods to see if you could have complied with all loan covenants, especially key ratios, if your loan had been in place before now.
5. If those results indicate future problems, schedule a visit with your banker and suggest more realistic covenants.

something really bad happens."

Given how heavily the U.S. banking industry is regulated, your banker's attitude makes sense. Banks aren't supposed to engage in high-risk investments that could endanger their customers' savings. Meanwhile, banks can't monitor their investments in companies like yours on a daily , or even frequent, basis. Loan covenants have evolved as banks' next-best safeguard, through monthly, quarterly, or annual regulation of key financial ratios and other essentials.

MYTH: Until your company is supersuccessful, you won't be able to qualify for better covenants, so why try to negotiate?

REALITY: Once a bank decides to give your company a loan, it's in the bank's interest to make the entire loan agreement as accurate as possible. But if you don't warn your banker that a covenant just won't work, how will he or she know?

"This is the stage to stop selling to your banker and, instead, start setting realistic expectations," explains Douglas Reynolds, a partner at the Boston law firm Peabody & Arnold. He and other experts agree that business owners won't jeopardize a loan simply by trying to negotiate covenant issues. If a requirement is inappropriate for your industry or your business, tell your banker why — before you sign a loan agreement. Be prepared with documentation (especially past financial records), as well as with suggestions about alternative standards your company could meet.

MYTH: If you've made all your loan payments on time, your banker won't really mind a slipup or two on a covenant.

REALITY: Don't kid yourself. If you anticipate falling out of compliance during any period that your banker monitors, you could wind up in hot water.

At the first sign of trouble, Douglas Fineberg, a banking consultant based in North Hampton, N.H., warns company owners to "*very realistically* assess the situation. If the problem is one of an extremely short term nature, and you're convinced you can correct it before you're due to report results to your bank, then you probably don't have to worry. But if you can't cure it fast, then you have to look for ways to minimize the situation."

Avoid methods of communication that might suggest you don't take the problem seriously. That means no quick notes or phone calls. "Ask your banker to come to your office to meet with you and your attorney

LINGUA BANKER

There are more potential covenants in a loan agreement than ingredients in a gourmet dinner. But here are some types of restrictions you may encounter:

- **Full disclosure.** "Banks were burned badly during the 1980s, when they often relied on information that turned out to be inaccurate or misleading," notes banking consultant Douglas Fineberg. Now most demand audited financial statements on an annual, quarterly, or even monthly basis. (That frequency is a hidden loan cost, since the more often you need audited statements, the higher your compliance costs.) Other covenants may spell out how soon you'll need to notify the bank of significant changes in circumstances, such as the loss of a major customer.
- **Salary caps.** Bankers want to prevent the top management from removing so much cash from the company that loans don't get repaid. Salary caps might be tied to a percent of sales or profits, or simply appear as a dollar limit.
- **Key ratios**. Bankers track various financial ratios to make certain your company can handle its loan payments. "You'll often see what's loosely called a liquidity ratio," says lawyer Douglas Reynolds. "This might calculate pretax income before debt payment and then compare it with whatever the company will need to service its debt—meaning the interest plus principal payments—and also be able to continue to operate." Other key ratios can vary widely; not all banks rely on the same formulas or definitions. You can probably expect some version of a quick ratio (cash plus cash equivalents and accounts receivable, divided by current liabilities) and a current ratio (current assets, including inventory, divided by current liabilities). The rules differ, but expect to see covenants approximating 1 to 1 for a quick ratio and 2 to 1 for a current ratio.
- **Net worth.** You may encounter a whole group of covenants about your company's (and sometimes your personal) net worth. The loan agreement often specifies a minimum value below which your company's net worth should not drop. You may also be tied to a debt-to-net-worth ratio.
- **Personal guarantee.** This is essential to many small-business loans. As soon as you prove your company's creditworthiness, negotiate to remove this covenant—fast.

and accountant," advises Fineberg. "Be prepared to give a full explanation of what's gone wrong and what you're prepared to do to correct it." It's a good idea to follow up on such a conversation in writing.

MYTH: You'll never escape from all these covenants.

REALITY: Once you have several banks competing to win you as a customers, it's much easier to negotiate less restrictive covenants. That's playing the best banking game of all: "Let's Make a Deal."

Inc.
August, 1997
Pages 99-100

QUESTIONS FOR CONSIDERATION:

1. What is a covenant and why do lenders often require them?
2. How might covenants also serve in certain ways to protect the interests of the borrower?

Name: ______________________ Professor: ______________________

Course: ______________________ Section: ______________________

Assignment 12
STOCKHOLDERS' EQUITY

Name of your company: ______________________

When you have completed this assignment, you should have a thorough understanding of the equity financing activities that your company has engaged in, both during the current period and over its life. Use the information in your firm's Annual Report to Stockholders and its SEC 10-K Report to complete this assignment. In addition, you will need to consult the most recent issue of *The Wall Street Journal* or the Sunday edition of your local newspaper.

COMPLETING THE ASSIGNMENT:

1. Identify the categories and amounts of your firm's capital stock. Some companies have more than one class of common stock (e.g., Class A common and Class B common). Similarly, some companies have more than one issue of preferred stock. Complete the following table for each class of your firm's common stock and each class of your firm's preferred stock. Clearly identify each class of stock.

	Number Of Shares (in 000s)			Par value (or stated value)
	Authorized	**Issued**	**Outstanding**	**per share**
Common stock:				
________	________	________	________	________
________	________	________	________	________
________	________	________	________	________
Preferred stock:				
________	________	________	________	________
________	________	________	________	________
________	________	________	________	________

2. Identify the changes in your firm's equity accounts that occurred during the most recent accounting period. Not all firms will have an entry for each item while some companies will have items that are not listed here.

	Amount on Most Recent Balance Sheet	Amount at End of Prior Year	Net Change in dollars	Net Change in percent
Preferred stock	________	________	______	______
Common stock	________	________	______	______
Additional paid-in capital (excess over par)	________	________	______	______
Deferred compensation	________	________	______	______
Cumulative translation adjustments	________	________	______	______
Retained earnings	________	________	______	______
Treasury stock	________	________	______	______
(other) ____________	________	________	______	______
Total stockholders' equity	________*	________*	______	______

*These amounts should match the totals on the balance sheet.

3. Briefly summarize the **significant** changes in stockholders' equity, if any, that occurred during the most recent year.

____

____

____

____

____

____

____

____

4. If your company had preferred stock outstanding at any time during the most recent year, indicate which of the following features apply.

	Yes	No
a. Cumulative	___	___
b. Participating	___	___
c. Redeemable	___	___
d. Convertible	___	___
e. Voting privileges	___	___

If your firm had no preferred stock outstanding, place a check mark in the space below.

______

f. For any of the characteristics above (except cumulative) that apply to your firm's preferred stock, indicate the specifics of that characteristic to your stock. For example, if it is convertible, under what terms can it be converted? (Hint: Most of this information will be in the notes.)

____

____

____

____

____

5. Indicate below whether your firm had treasury stock at the end of the current period and/or at the end of the prior period.

	Current Balance Sheet	Prior Balance Sheet	Percent Change
a. Number of shares	________	________	______
b. Dollar amount	________	________	______
c. Is it reported at its **cost**? (If not, ignore the next question.)	________	________	
d. What was the average price* paid to acquire the treasury stock?	________	________	______

*Average price = total cost/number of shares

6. Did your company issue stock, either common or preferred, during the most recent year? (This is reported on the statement of stockholders' equity, if one is included in the financial statements. Otherwise, look on the statement of cash flows under Financing Activities and/or on a supplementary schedule that sometimes accompanies the statement of cash flows.)

   _______ Yes

   _______ No

   If yes, identify the number of shares issued of each type of stock, par value (if any), and total dollar amount received from each issue.

	Type of Stock	Number of Shares Issued	Par Value (per share)	Total Dollar Amount
a.	____________________	______________	___________	_______________
b.	____________________	______________	___________	_______________
c.	____________________	______________	___________	_______________
d.	____________________	______________	___________	_______________

7. Does the firm have any executive stock options outstanding at its most recent balance sheet date?

   ____

   If yes, by what percent would the number of common shares outstanding increase if all executive stock options were exercised? Show your clearly labeled work in the space provided below.

   __________%

Learning Note: The following three ratios are computed to provide information about a company's common stock price and about the company's dividend practices. The computational formula and the information content of each ratio is explained below.

a. **Price-earnings ratio (commonly referred to as the P/E ratio):** *current market price of common stock ÷ diluted earnings per share.* This ratio measures investors' expectations about a company's future earnings. If investors' are paying a high price for the stock, this indicates they expect significant growth in future earnings and the P/E ratio will be high (e.g., in the 30s or higher). If investors will only pay a low price for the stock, they are indicating pessimism about future earnings growth and the P/E ratio will be low (e.g., in single digits).

b. **Dividend payout ratio:** *total cash dividends paid on common stock ÷ net income minus preferred dividends.* This ratio reveals the percentage of the income earned by the common stock that was paid out in common dividends. In other words, it yields the portion of earnings per share that is paid out as dividends.

c. **Dividend yield ratio:** *cash dividend per share of common stock ÷ market price per share of common stock.* This ratio measures the cash return per share of common stock. (Note that the total return on a share of stock would include both the cash dividend plus or minus the change in the market price of the share.)

8. Compute your firm's price-earnings ratio, dividend payout ratio, and dividend yield ratio.

   a. Price-earnings ratio = $\dfrac{\text{current market price of common stock*}}{\text{(diluted) earnings per share}}$

      i. **Price-earnings ratio** = ------------------------------------ = ___________

*The current market price of your firm's common stock can be obtained from the most recent issue of *The Wall Street Journal* (published every weekday and available in most libraries). You will find the stock prices in *The Wall Street Journal's* Section C. Alternatively, the Sunday editions of most local newspapers carry a summary of end-of-the-week corporate stock prices.

ii. Based on the guidelines from the learning note on the prior page, what does your firm's price-earnings ratio tend to indicate about investors' expectations regarding the company's future earnings?

____

____

____

____

____

b. Dividend payout ratio = $\dfrac{\text{total cash dividends on common stock}}{\text{net income minus preferred dividends}}$

i. **Dividend payout ratio** = ------------------------------------ = __________

ii. Assuming the dividend payout ratio you just computed has been fairly constant over recent years, briefly explain what this implies about the company's dividend payment policy.

____

____

____

____

____

c. Dividend yield ratio = $\dfrac{\text{cash dividend per share of common stock}}{\text{current market price per share of common stock*}}$

i. **Dividend yield ratio** = ------------------------------------ = __________

*The current market price of your firm's common stock can be obtained from the most recent issue of *The Wall Street Journal* (published every weekday and available in most libraries). You will find the stock prices in *The Wall Street Journal's* Section C. Alternatively, the Sunday editions of most local newspapers carry a summary of end-of-the-week corporate stock prices.

ii. Assuming the dividend yield ratio you just computed has been fairly constant over recent years, briefly explain what this reveals about the cash return an owner receives on his/her investment each year. Do you believe this is a satisfactory return on a stockholder's investment? What other source of return (besides dividends) do stockholders earn on their investment?

Reading 12

What's Driving Return on Equity?

You Need To Look Beyond The Single Number To Understand Why ROE Is Booming

By RICHARD S. TEITELBAUM
Reporter Associates: Kimberly Seals Mcdonald and Ed Brown

There's never been anything like it. By any number of measures, return on shareholder equity, traditionally the single most important and widely noted benchmark of corporate performance, has sprinted over the past several years to its loftiest level in U.S. history. Look at a few different ROE numbers and gape in wonder: The S&P 400 index of industrials sports a dizzying ROE of 22%. The 30 companies that make up the Dow Jones industrial average finished with a year-end return of 20.5%. And our own FORTUNE 500 list of America's largest corporations — handicapped compared with the others because it includes so many service companies — weighs in with an aggregate ROE of 14.6%. "There is no precedent for ROE anywhere like this," says James Gipson, president of Pacific Financial Research, a money management firm in Beverly Hills. "We are in uncharted territory."

To keep all those numbers in perspective, consider that back in 1978, a not-so-well-known investor named Warren E. Buffett penned a lengthy article for FORTUNE in which he opined that return on equity was not likely to stray from the 12% level for very long. Can you blame him for thinking so? During the first nine years of the FORTUNE 500, from 1956 to 1964, when it tracked only industrial companies, ROE averaged 11.04%. The next ten years, from 1965 to 1974, it averaged only slightly more, 11.97%. Even during a period bedeviled by inflation, from 1975 to 1984, the 500's ROE only sped up to an average of 13.26%.

Why focus on ROE? Well, consider the elegantly simple dynamics of the ratio, most easily defined as profits divided by shareholders' equity. Because it shows the amount of earnings produced by each dollar of equity, ROE gives investors a markedly handy gauge with which to measure management performance. What better way to judge a CEO than on his ability to make use of shareholders' funds? Bear in mind that it's the promise of future returns implicit in this benchmark that makes it so beguiling to investors. Earn a consistent ROE of 20% and, heck, keep your dividend check: After a quick four years, the value of my investment will have doubled. The boom in return on equity goes a long way toward explaining the bullish tenor of today's market.

Like any statistic, ROE has its limitations. You need to be careful when weighing ROE for different industries. In some cases, accounting practices distort results and yield apple-and-orange comparisons. For example, a drug company's biggest investment, R&D, gets treated as an expense instead of an asset. This reduces shareholders' equity, thus increasing leverage, and the slim asset base keeps turnover high. The effect is to bolster the industry's average ROE. Auto companies and some computer makers had their returns hammered by accounting changes in 1992, though they have since broken the 15% mark. And the business cycle always affects industries differently. Bank ROEs tanked in the 1990-91 recession and have since bounced back smartly, while noncyclical drug companies navigated those years with nary a hiccup.

The big question is: Are U.S. businesses's racy ROE numbers sustainable? The short answer: probably not, certainly not forever. But to understand why, you have to smoke out the several factors that have been driving ROE. Back in 1903, an E.I. du Pont de Nemours senior accounting executive, Donaldson Brown, came up with a concept that helps do just that. He figured that return on equity can be arrived at by multiplying profit margin (profits as a percent of sales) and turnover (sales as a percent of assets, or, to put it another way, the rate at which a company's resources are turned into sales). Later, Du Pont accountants discovered that another variable, leverage (assets as a multiple of equity), could be added to the formula to factor in the effect of financing costs on returns. Apply the overall formula today and you find all sorts of salutary tidings for the nation's ROE: Leverage and turnover are high, and profit margins are going as wild as sophomores on spring break.

DU PONT'S FORMULA FOR ROE

PROFIT MARGIN x	*TURNOVER x*	*LEVERAGE =*	*ROE*
(Profits/Sales)	(Sales/Assets)	(Assets/Equity)	

THE FORTUNE 500'S ROE

1994:	*5.04%*	*x*	*.446*	*x*	*6.399*	*=*	*14.4%*
1995:	*5.20%*	*x*	*.447*	*x*	*6.285*	*=*	*14.6%*

Great run-ups in corporate return on equity, as you might expect, always take place against a backdrop of economic growth, typically near the peak of a business cycle. That's true now. But today's big news is that the current strong profits are largely a result of powerfully expanding margins. Look at this data from Investors Management Group, a Des Moines money management firm: So far in the 1990s, the growth in profits, at 11.5%, has far outstripped the growth in sales, shuffling along at just 5.6%. Put another way: Since 1990, nearly half of all profit growth has come from fatter margins. Compare that with past decades: In the 1950s, just 12.6% of profit growth came from margin expansion. Margins actually shrank on average in the 1960s and 1970s. And in the 1980s, a puny 4.3% of profit growth came from margin expansion. Such rising profit margins — the first part of the Du Pont equation — have, of course, goosed ROE, proportionately.

The reasons for corporate America's obsession with the bottom line are easy to fathom. For starters, there was a lot of fat to cut. As senior managing director James Paulsen of Investors Management Group puts it: "Much of the success of the 1990s is just cutting through the bloat of the past five decades." Another secular cause has probably been U.S. businesses' $288 billion of computer-related spending over the past six years. Why? Computers increase the efficiency of back-office jobs, cutting expenses and pushing up profit margins.

Then, too, businesses scarcely seem to have any other choice. The 1990s is a decade of low growth, low expectations, and scant consumer excitement. Core inflation has languished at a measly 3.5% since 1990, helping to strip companies of their ability to make price increases stick. Witness the price wars, or at least skirmishes, that have been popping up on various goods from diapers to computers to toothpaste whenever businesses attempt to raise sales in today's environment. And the anti-inflationary predisposition of Alan Greenspan & Co. should ensure that this remains the norm.

The upside to our low-inflation era: Corporate America has been benefiting from the lowest long-term interest rates in over a generation. The yield on 30-year Treasury bonds, 7.9% at the end of 1989, had fallen to just over 5.9% by the end of 1995, although it has since climbed back to 6.7%. Result: According to Sanford C. Bernstein & Co., the average after-tax cost of debt has fallen from 2.3% in 1991 to just 1.4%. And that, too, has fed into fattening margins.

That ROE has soared even as inflation has remained low is especially impressive, because inflation itself is one of the things that's boosted ROE in the past. Back in 1979 the economy was growing at a 2.9% annual rate and ROE hit 16.5%. But a key catalyst was an inflation rate of 11.3%. How so? Consider the Du Pont equation: Sales, riding the run-up in prices, gallop away. But assets on the balance sheet, which tend to get replaced gradually over time, lag in nominal amounts. Result: Turnover, or sales divided by assets, rockets, sending overall return on equity skyward.

What's happening with turnover today — the second part of the Du Pont formula? Just-in-time inventory practices are still having their beneficent effect, allowing companies to rev sales higher with fewer assets. Here's proof: The turnover of FORTUNE's top ten corporations rose from 0.757 in 1990 to 0.796 in 1995. Sounds like small potatoes? Bear in mind that with this type of equation, the percentage change in ROE will equal the percentage rise in any one of its variables. Thus, that 5.1% change in the ratio would have raised a 10% ROE to 10.5% — not a negligible number when you consider that the difference between a 10% and 15% ROE spells the difference between mediocrity and stardom.

Further widespread improvements in turnover will be hard to come by — inventory-to-sales ratios, in fact, have come up off their lows in the past two years, and rising inventories reduce turnover. But companies like Dana Corp., America's largest independent supplier of auto parts and systems, are still trimming. Inventory as a percentage of sales fell at Dana from 14% in 1990 to 11% in 1995, even as it acquired less efficient plants and businesses around the globe. How lean are companies running? Just recall how GM's North American operations were quickly brought to a grinding halt by a strike at two brake factories in Dayton.

To turn back to the ROE formula, we've nailed down two of the three variables: Margins have soared; turnover is up. The last part is leverage, or assets divided by stockholders' equity. Assets have been rising modestly, as you'd expect in a slow-growing economy. But equity is going in the other direction, as vast amounts get scorched off the balance sheets of corporate America through restructurings, accounting charges, and stock buybacks. Result: higher leverage.

First, behold the increasingly familiar big-ticket restructuring — the method of choice for companies seeking to dispose of unwanted staff and sub-par businesses. The charge associated with such upheaval can work its way through a company's financial statements like a tornado through a Midwestern trailer park. It starts on the income statement, of course, where the company posts a massive loss for the year. But the amount over and above operating income has its longer-lasting impact when it touches down on the balance sheet. There it gets subtracted from retained earnings, and in so doing blows away huge swaths of shareholders' equity, setting the stage for higher ROE in the future. Look at the results for IBM, which booked $24.2 billion in pretax restructuring charges in 1991, 1992, and 1993. Shareholders' equity, largely as a result, has fallen from $42.8 billion in 1990 to $22.4 billion in 1995, making it a cinch for IBM to sport a smart return of 19%.

Blood-soaked restructurings, of course, haven't been the only the source of the slaughter of stockholders' equity. Witness the innocuously named accounting standards — SFAS (statement of financial accounting standards) No. 106 and No. 112. These have prompted companies to write down their assets to more realistically value the promises they make to workers about such things as health care, insurance, and other benefits after retirement. In fact, equity really was overstated in previous years, and the impact of this reality check on balance sheets was startling. GM took a $33.1 billion pretax SFAS 106 charge in 1992, a move that will bolster the carmaker's ROE — a fat 30% in 1995 — for years to come. The one-two punch of these two varieties of charges moves us into the realm of truly gargantuan numbers. Jack T. Ciesielski of the Analyst's Accounting Observer, a research service, toted up the combined effects of restructuring and accounting charges on the Dow Jones industrials from 1991 through 1994. Total equity consumed: $96 billion, or 35% of the amount outstanding at the end of the period.

One final force pushing down shareholders' equity is the phenomenon of stock-buyback programs, a sort of corporate cannibalism with its own simple, self-reinforcing logic. It works like this: A company buys back stock; shareholders' equity declines; return on equity increases; future buybacks become even more alluring. Since 1990, General Electric has engaged in two such bouts of stock buybacks. The first retired 4% of the outstanding stock; the second, 3%. GE is not alone: US. stock buybacks have amounted to an estimated 1.8% of market capitalization per year, on average, since 1989. Think of it from the company's perspective. Why search for investment or business opportunities with above-average returns when an enterprise that you are intimately familiar with — your own company — can so easily furnish the same? Managements that buy their own stock have looked pretty smart in the rising markets of the 1990s. GE's two repurchases were done at average prices of $33.80 and $58.50. The stock recently traded at $77.

Can the ROE run-up continue? Some very smart people say it can and will: Strategists and economists, brokers and buy-siders alike, are proclaiming a sea change in America's corporate tidings, and nowhere is it written that they can't be right. But a more conservative — and more realistic — approach would be to simply enjoy it while it lasts, and to remember that ROE, like the market itself, can go down as well as up.

Fortune
April 29, 1996
Pages 271-276

Questions for Consideration:

1. What factors have caused return on equity to increase so significantly in recent years?

2. Do you think further changes in return on equity are likely in the future? Why or why not?

Name: ______________________ Professor: ______________________

Course: ______________________ Section: ______________________

Assignment 13
SEGMENT INFORMATION

Name of your company ______________________

Most large publicly-traded companies have operations in more than one line of business, or operate in various geographic areas, or have different parts of the business subject to differing levels of regulation. The purpose of this assignment is to understand the component parts (i.e., segments) of your company's operations. Are some segments growing more rapidly than others? Which are generating most of the company's sales and profits?

To help financial statement users make better judgments about the company as a whole, GAAP require that companies split out certain specific information by segment. To meet these disclosure requirements, firms usually organize their financial results into two, three, or four segments. Seldom does a company report more than five segments. Usually this information is reported near the end of the notes section. In this assignment you will focus primarily on segment revenues, segment assets, and segment profit.

> **NOTE:** Some firms report that they operate as a single segment. If this is the situation for your firm, you will not be able to complete this assignment. Ask your instructor if he/she would like you to use a different company for this part of ***The Financial Reporting Project.***

COMPLETING THE ASSIGNMENT:

1. Find and read your firm's segment information in the notes to the financial statements. (It's usually one of the last notes). Answer the questions below.

   a. What is the basis your firm has chosen upon which to report segments? (Mark one below.)

   ___ Products or services ___ Geography ___ Regulatory environment ___ Other

   b. What are the names of your firm's segments and what are the primary types of products that are sold in each? Complete the table on the next page.

Segment Name	Types of Products Sold

c. To determine whether management is "growing" one or more of the segments faster than the others, complete the following table by using the data provided in the notes. Divide (1) the segment's total expenditures for long-lived assets by (2) the segment's total assets. Do this for each segment for up to three years.

	Total expenditures for long-lived assets ÷ total assets		
Segment Name	**Most recent year**	**Next most recent year**	**Next most recent year**
______________	_____%	_____%	_____%
______________	_____	_____	_____
______________	_____	_____	_____
______________	_____	_____	_____
______________	_____	_____	_____

d. Does your analysis in part (c.) indicate that management is "growing" one or more segments more rapidly than the others? Why might this be? Discuss.

____

____

____

____

____

2. Complete the table of segment information below. List the segment profit, segment assets, and return on segment assets (of each segment) for the most recent year and two prior years. List the most recent year's information first. Divide column A by column B to obtain the return on segment assets.

		(A)	(B)	(A)/(B)
Segment Names	**Year**	**Segment Profit**	**Segment Assets**	**Return on Segment Assets**
a. ________	____	________	________	________
	____	________	________	________
	____	________	________	________
b. ________	____	________	________	________
	____	________	________	________
	____	________	________	________
c. ________	____	________	________	________
	____	________	________	________
	____	________	________	________
d. ________	____	________	________	________
	____	________	________	________
	____	________	________	________
e. ________	____	________	________	________
	____	________	________	________
	____	________	________	________
f. ________	____	________	________	________
	____	________	________	________
	____	________	________	________

3. Discuss the results of your segment profitability analysis. What trends do you observe? Are some segments performing better than others? What segment-related questions would you ask of management if you had the opportunity? Might overall profitability be enhanced by reallocating assets to some segments and away from others? Does management address "segment strategies" in the Management Discussion and Analysis section of the Annual Report? What do they say? Discuss and explain.

> **Learning Note:** To better understand profit results, analysts often split return on assets into its two component parts: profit margin and asset turnover. The profit margin reveals the number of pennies out of each sales dollar that a company retains (as profit) after paying all of its expenses. Asset turnover reveals how many times during the accounting period that those pennies were earned. Ideally, companies would prefer to have high profit margin **and** high asset turnover. In reality, companies vary widely in their combinations of margin and turnover. Similarly, segments can vary widely in their margins and turnover. A segment's profit margin multiplied times its asset turnover equals the return on segment assets for that segment.
>
> A segment's **profit margin** is computed as: segment profit ÷ total segment revenues. A segment's **asset turnover** is computed as: total segment revenues ÷ segment assets.

4. To understand more about how your company's segment profits are generated, compute the profit margin, asset turnover, and return on segment assets for each of your firm's segments. Use the formulas from the Learning Note (and shown below) for your computations of each segment's profit margin, asset turnover, and return on segment assets.

	Segment Profit Margin	**x**	**Segment Asset Turnover**	**=**	**Return on Segment Assets**
	segment profit / total segment revenues	x	total segment revenues / segment assets	=	return on segment assets
Segment					
a. ____________	______		______		______
b. ____________	______		______		______
c. ____________	______		______		______
d. ____________	______		______		______
e. ____________	______		______		______
f. ____________	______		______		______

5. Discuss the comparative profit margins and asset turnover that you computed for your company's segments. Do they differ markedly or they all about the same? If there are significant differences, is there anything about the nature of the various products in the different segments that would tend to explain the differences you found? Discuss.

Reading 13

Learn To Play The Earnings Game (And Wall Street Will Love You)

The pressure to report smooth, ever higher earnings has never been fiercer. You don't want to miss the consensus estimate by a penny — and you don't have to.

By JUSTIN FOX

In January, for the 41st time in the 42 quarters since it went public, Microsoft reported earnings that met or beat Wall Street estimates. The 36 brokerage analysts who make the estimates were, as a group, quite happy about this — the 57 cents per share announced by the software giant was above their consensus of 51 cents, but not so far above as to make them look stupid. Investors were happy too, bidding the already high-priced shares of the company up 4% the first trading day after the announcement.

In short, for yet another quarter, Microsoft had kept its comfortable spot in the innermost sphere of corporate paradise. This is what chief executives and chief financial officers dream of: quarter after quarter after blessed quarter of not disappointing Wall Street. Sure, they dream about other things too — megamergers, blockbuster new products, global domination. But the simplest, most visible, most merciless measure of corporate success in the 1990s has become this one: Did you make your earnings last quarter?

This is new. Executives of public companies have always strived to live up to investors' expectations, and keeping earnings rising smoothly and predictably has long been seen as the surest way to do that. But it's only in the past decade, with the rise to prominence of the consensus earnings estimates compiled first in the early 1970s by I/B/E/S (it stands for Institutional Brokers Estimate System) and now also by competitors Zacks, First Call, and Nelson's, that those expectations have become so explicit. Possibly as a result, companies are doing a better job of hitting their targets: For an unprecedented 16 consecutive quarters, more S&P 500 companies have beat the consensus earnings estimates than missed them.

Microsoft's prodigious record of beating expectations is due in large part to the company's prodigious growth, from annual revenues of $198 million at the time of its IPO in 1986 to more than $9 billion now. It also helps that it dominates its industry. But even the Microsofts of the business world have a few tricks up their sleeve. The most obvious is to manage earnings. "Managing earnings" has a pejorative, slightly sleazy ring to it, but even at the most respected of companies, accounting and business decisions are regularly made with smoothing or temporarily boosting earnings in mind. Not all are as up front about it as General Electric, where executives say openly that they don't think their company would be as popular with investors if its profits weren't so consistent and predictable. But neither can it be a complete coincidence that of the top ten companies on FORTUNE's 1997 Most Admired list, seven — Coca-Cola, Merck, Microsoft, Johnson & Johnson, Intel, Pfizer, and Procter & Gamble — have missed fewer than five quarters in the past five years, according to I/B/E/S (and two of the other three don't have any earnings estimates to meet).

Meeting the estimates is made easier by the fact that they're not set in a vacuum. Analysts rely heavily on guidance from companies to form their forecasts, and companies have in recent years figured out that it pays to guide the analysts to a lower rather than a higher number. At least partly as a result of this expectational interplay, the price of missing a quarter has risen sharply, particularly among high-priced growth stocks. In the growth stock fraternity, "missing by a penny" now implies the height of corporate boneheadedness — that is, if you couldn't find that extra penny to keep Wall Street happy, then your company must really be in trouble, and since missing by a penny is already going to send your stock plummeting, you're better off missing by a dime or two and saving those earnings for the next quarter.

Microsoft missed by a penny once — back in 1988, when such behavior was not yet considered unbearably gauche. Nowadays its executives treat analysts to a constant patter of cautionary and even downbeat words about the future that the analysts say is a mix of genuine paranoia and astute expectations management. That's what [Microsoft] CFO Mike Brown did, along with the usual warnings about slower growth ahead, during his regular quarterly conference call after the January 17 earnings release. He told the hundreds of analysts, money managers, and journalists listening in that earnings would be "more than a nickel, less than a dime" higher than predicted for the current quarter, and another penny higher in the next.

How did he know this? That involves something that looks a lot like earnings management — although not of the sort that provokes penalties from the Securities and Exchange Commission or nasty newspaper articles about inflated profits. Starting around the unveiling of Windows 95 in August 1995, Microsoft has followed a uniquely conservative method of accounting for the software it ships — deferring recognition of large chunks of revenue from a product until long after the product is sold. The reasoning is that when somebody buys software in 1996, they're also buying the right to upgrades and customer support in 1997 and 1998. If it hadn't been for the new accounting technique, the company would have had to report a sharp rise in profits in the latter half of 1995, then a sharp drop in the first half of 1996 — a turn of events that might have sent its stock price reeling — instead of the smoothly rising earnings that it did post. By the end of 1996, Microsoft had taken in $1.1 billion in "unearned revenue" that it had yet to recognize on its income statements. "Because of this, they know what they've got in the bag from one quarter to the next," says Marshall Senk, a Robertson Stephens analyst who follows the company. Which leads him to conclude that "Microsoft does a better job of leveraging accounting — I would almost say it's a competitive weapon — than anybody else in the industry."

Microsoft treasurer Greg Maffei doesn't like this interpretation. "I'm a financial officer of this company, and I would be in deep doo-doo with the SEC if that was what was driving our revenue recognition policies," he says. "Our revenue recognition policies are driven by GAAP." Which isn't quite true. In fact, GAAP — the Generally Accepted Accounting Principles companies follow in preparing financial statements — may in this area be driven by Microsoft. Virtually no other software company does its accounting the way Microsoft does, but standards setters, egged on by the industry leader, are starting to push in that direction.

That's how GAAP works. It's constantly changing and evolving, particularly in businesses that haven't been around for long. This is only natural, but it can be maddening for people trying to understand what a company's reported earnings really mean. "With industries that haven't been in the market before, you tend to see a lot of monkey business because accountants, even if well intentioned, don't know what the standards are," says Martin Fridson, high-yield debt strategist at Merrill Lynch and a financial statement analysis guru. "Underwriters of small companies and people who make a living doing IPOs are very conscious of the markets inability to see what the correct measure are." Add that confusion to the general cacophony of accounting quirks and judgement calls in financial statements, and you begin to realize that earnings are nothing but a vague, approximate measure anyway.

One of modern accounting's guiding principles is that of matching revenues and expenses over time. That's why the cost of building a factory that will be churning out cars for 20 years gets expensed over those 20 years, not when the money is actually spent. But such matching requires making all sorts of guesses an estimates about the future. These judgements — how much to set aside for potential loan losses, what rate of return to expect on pension fund, over how many years to spread out the cost of a factory — make earnings a better reflection of the long term economic health of a company. They also provide ample room for managers to fudge. This is why financial analysts and money managers are supposed to know how to look beyond a company's bottom line to find the true economic value in its balance sheet or cash flow statement or, best of all, the footnotes to its financial statements. In the bull market of the past 15 years, however, analytic rigor hasn't always been required to make good stock picks. "Nobody's paying attention," says Robert Olstein Financial Alert fund.

If Microsoft is the archetype of a hugely successful company trying to tone its earnings down so people don't get their expectations too high, Boston Chicken bespeaks an altogether different and more common phenomenon. It is a business that isn't successful yet but has used accounting to help convince investors that it already is, or at least will be soon. This has enabled it to raise more than $800 million in stock and convertible debt offerings, money which has been essential not only to the company's rapid growth — from 175 Boston Chicken restaurants when it went public in one of the decade's hottest IPOs in November 1993 to 1,100 restaurants (rechristened Boston Markets) and 325 Einstein Brothers and Noah's bagel stores today — but to its very survival. That's because, economically speaking, Boston Chicken is still a big money loser, as probably can be expected of a startup restaurant chain. All the losses, however, have been incurred by "financed area developers," or FADS, which is Boston Chicken lingo for large-scale franchisees that act a lot like subsidiaries but aren't. If they were, their losses would have to be reported on Boston Chicken's income statement (they are instead disclosed, on an annual basis only, deep in the text of the company's SEC filings). The FADs get 75% of their startup capital in loans from Boston Chicken, and with that money they pay the company the royalties, franchise fees, and interest that allow it to report ever-rising profits. Once the restaurants start making money, Boston Chicken exercises its right to convert the loans into equity, officially dubbing the FADs subsidiaries and allowing their profits to flow to its bottom line.

That's the plan, at least, as outlined with somewhat more delicacy in the company's 1993 annual report. And so far it has worked. Sure, business publications have printed nasty articles about the company, accounting professors have warned their students about it, and short sellers have lined up in droves to place bets that its stock price will crash. But Boston Chicken's stock price has more than held its own. It sure doesn't hurt, analysts and money managers say, that not only is Boston Chicken able to report earnings every quarter, but those earnings have so far never failed to meet or surpass analysts' expectations — even though those analysts all know that the earnings in no significant way reflect how the company is doing. "It's a very smart strategy," says Michael Moe, a growth stock strategist at Montgomery Securities. "It has made enormous amounts of capital available to them at an attractive price that most companies can only dream of."

Boston Chicken CFO Mark Stephens says his company was structured not to please Wall Street but to provide flexibility and motivate its franchisees. But he acknowledges that "a byproduct of where we are with the structure is that we have a public entity with an earnings complexion that is attractive." He adds: "It's like sausage. I love the product; just don't show me how it's made."

Is there evidence of widespread earnings management? You bet. Looking at 17 years of I/B/E/S data on more than 1,000 companies, Jeff Payne of the University of Mississippi and Sean Robb of Canada's Wilfrid Laurier University found an unmistakable pattern of using accruals (i.e., judgement calls) to manage earnings upward if they were below the analysts' consensus and a somewhat less pronounced trend of managing them downward if they were above the consensus.

General Electric, a company whose name invariably comes up when you ask Wall Streeters about earnings management, says it does what it does because the stock market demands it. "We think consistency of earnings and no surprises is very important for us," says Dennis Dammerman, the company's CFO. "We're a very complex, diverse company that no one from the outside looking in can reasonably be expected to understand in complete detail; so our story to the investing world is, we have a lot of diverse businesses, and when you put them all together they produce consistent, reliable earnings growth." And if something inconsistent comes along — say, a one-time gain from selling off a factory —"we have a pretty consistent record of saying, 'Okay, we're going to take these large gains and offset them with discretionary decisions, with restructurings.'"

These tactics have helped GE meet or beat expectations every quarter but one in the past five years, and they certainly haven't hurt it among investors, even skeptical ones. "They are using all sorts of techniques to smooth earnings," says Howard Schilit, whose Center for Financial Research and Analysis keeps institutional investors posted on companies whose earnings numbers may be biding business troubles. "If I wrote that to my clients, there would be a big yawn."

Another investor favorite that produces awfully smooth earnings is Coca-Cola, which in the third quarter of last year took advantage of $520 million in one-time gains from a settlement with the IRS and the sale of some bottling operations to recognize $500 million in supposedly one-time hits to earnings. One of those hits, $200 million used to reduce the inventories of soft drink concentrate at bottling companies, was explained as a move to free up bottlers' capital but was seen by some as an admission that Coke had been shipping concentrate early to artificially boost earnings. That hurt the company's stock price for a few months, but by taking the charge Coke gave itself the option of using inventory buildup at its bottlers to pad profits later. "When they pull it out in 1998 or 1999 to keep up their 19% or 20% earnings growth, everyone will have forgotten," says Roy Burry, who follows Coke for Oppenheimer & Co.

Will everyone really forget? If financial markets are in fact efficient, economic reality will in the long run win out over accounting games. But the long run can seem awfully far away when you've got a posse of analysts breathing down your neck every three months. Many corporate executives also seem to think investors take earnings numbers at face value; they write outraged letters to the Financial Accounting Standards Board, accounting's top rule-making body, whenever it proposes a change that might reduce reported earnings. "They obviously don't believe in efficient markets," says Neel Foster, a FASB member and former treasurer of Compaq Computer. "Academic evidence shows that generally, accounting changes don't result in changes in stock prices. But it also shows that people that make greater disclosures generally have a lower cost of capital. They don't believe that either."

Even this doesn't explain why some companies seem to persist in managing earnings in the face of Wall Street disbelief. Food maker H.J. Heinz grew rapidly during the 1980s but has since needed repeated asset sales and other special items to keep earnings steady — and its stock has lagged. Last June the company announced quarterly earnings of 45 cents a share but failed to mention that four of those cents came from the sale of a magazine and two pet food brands. It was "immaterial." a company spokesman says now, but it nevertheless infuriated some analysts, who found out only when they received the annual report a month later. It didn't help the stock price either, although the stock later bounced back on rumors of a major restructuring.

What might motivate such corporate behavior? One answer is money. High-level executives like to get paid a lot, and it so happens that many bonus plans — including the one at Heinz — are built around meeting earnings targets. The rise of performance related bonuses has taken earnings tweaking to new heights, say some market watchers. There's no reliable measure of such activity, but one rough gauge, comparing profits reported to the Internal Revenue Service by U.S. corporations with profits reported to shareholders (the measure that counts for bonuses) by companies on the S&P 500, gives a clue. It shows some wild relative swings in S&P earnings in the late 1980s and early 1990s, probably a result of big corporations using one-time charges to pay for restructuring costs like plant closures. This write-off binge ended in 1994, which could mean either that earnings quality is getting better or that companies are coasting to ever higher earnings now because they hid ongoing costs back then.

> It so happens that many executive bonus plans are built around meeting earnings targets.

While there's no conclusive proof that managing earnings is on the rise, it is undeniable that the game is being played more aggressively than ever. This isn't necessarily bad: "The good side of what a lot of people call the game of managing expectations is that companies realize that they have to give better guidance to the market as to what their prospects are." Says Ed Keon, senior vice president of marketing at I/B/E/S.

The downside of giving better guidance — apart from the hours of valuable-to-management time that it eats up — is that the investors most interested in the estimates are not exactly the well-run corporation's best friend. They are the momentum guys — mutual fund managers and hedge fund jockeys and individual investors — who jump on the bandwagon when a company's earnings growth is accelerating and beating the analysts' estimates, and jump off the second it misses a quarter.

"When it stops, they sell — you cannot break this algorithm," says a resigned Eric Benhamou, chief executive of 3Com Corp., which lost $7 billion in market value in a matter of weeks this year as it became known that its earnings for the quarter ended February 28 would not meet analysts' expectations.

The moral of the story: Unless you're a trader, ignore the short-term kabuki that the companies and the analysts perform for each other, but educate yourself about the accounting games that companies play. If enough investors did, it could mean that the smartest earnings and expectations management strategy of the 2000s will be — don't bother.

Fortune
March 31, 1997
Page 77-80

Questions for Consideration:

1. Does this article give you more confidence, or less confidence, in the financial reports of the companies mentioned in the article? Why?
2. Does earnings management (as described in this article) increase or decrease risk to those who rely on financial statement information? Discuss.

Name: ______________________________ Professor: ______________________

Course: ______________________________ Section: ______________________

Assignment 14
THE CASH FLOW STATEMENT

Name of your company ____

The purpose of this assignment is to understand the information presented on your company's cash flow statement. This financial statement is the only one that is **not** based on accrual accounting. It is a simple report of how much cash flowed into the company and how much cash flowed out. You will compare and contrast your company's cash flows from operating, financing, and investing activities.

COMPLETING THE ASSIGNMENT:

1. Indicate with a check mark in the appropriate space below whether your firm's cash flow statement was prepared using the direct approach or the indirect approach.

   a. Direct approach _____

   > If the first line under Operating Activities reads "Cash received from customers," or something similar, the direct approach is being used.

   b. Indirect approach _____

   > If the first line under Operating Activities reads "Net income," or something similar, the indirect approach is being used.

2. Does the net "change in cash" (sometimes labeled change in cash and cash equivalents) as reported on the cash flow statement match the change in cash balance reported on the comparative balance sheets for the most recent two year period?

   Yes ____ No ____ Amount of change(s) $________________________

> **Learning Note:** The linkage of an item on one financial statement to an item reported on a different financial statement is referred to as *financial statement articulation.*

3. Unless a firm issued significant amounts of equity or debt (e.g., stocks or bonds) during a year, operating activities should be the largest source of cash. If operating activities aren't generating a significant amount of cash from year to year the firm may be headed for trouble. A company that is regularly generating cash from investing activities also may be headed for trouble (i.e., the company may be selling off assets to pay its bills).

   a. Prepare a summary of your firm's cash flows for (up to) six years. There should be three years of data on the statement of cash flows. There may be additional years summarized in the Financial Highlights section. Report as many years as you can but not more than six.

SUMMARY OF CASH FLOWS
(in millions of dollars)

Category	Most Recent Year	Prior Years (label each column below)				
		_____	_____	_____	_____	_____
Operating activities	_____	_____	_____	_____	_____	_____
Investing activities	_____	_____	_____	_____	_____	_____
Financing activities	_____	_____	_____	_____	_____	_____
Net change in cash during year	_____	_____	_____	_____	_____	_____

   b. What do you conclude from the information above? Does the company appear to be generating a healthy cash flow from operations over the years or is it depending on cash from other sources to pay its bills? If cash from operations is often negative, it is a particularly bad sign. It means that every day when the company opens for business some of its cash "leaks out."

____

____

____

____

____

____

____

4. Usually, a company's cash outflow for investing activities is supplied by cash generated from operating activities and financing activities. Was this true for your firm in recent years?

   a. Determine the amounts and fill in the schedule below.

COMPARISON OF CASH INFLOW FROM OPERATING ACTIVITIES PLUS FINANCING ACTIVITIES TO CASH OUTFLOW FROM INVESTING ACTIVITIES (in millions of dollars)

	Most Recent Year	Prior Years (label each column below)				
		______	______	______	______	______
i. Cash generated (used) by operating activities plus financing activities	______	______	______	______	______	______
ii. Cash generated (used) by investing activities	______	______	______	______	______	______

iii. Is the cash provided by operating activities and financing activities together roughly equal to the amount of cash consumed by investing activities in each year? Answer "yes" or "no" for each year. (More than one "no" may indicate that further inquiry into cash flow is necessary.)

______ ______ ______ ______ ______ ______

b. Summarize your findings regarding part a. on the previous page. In general, is the *usual* situation occurring for your firm during the years studied? Are cash outflows from investing activities being adequately covered by cash inflows from operating activities and financing activities? Discuss.

Learning Note: Three ratios often are computed to assess the cash flow results of a firm. The computational formula and information content of each ratio is given below.

a. **Cash-based return on assets:** *net cash flow from operating activities ÷ average total assets.* This ratio is the cash-based equivalent of the accrual-based return on assets. In each case, the intent is to compare the results of operations to the amount of assets used to generate that result.

b. **Cash flows to current maturities of long-term debt:** *net cash flow from operating activities ÷ current maturities of long-term debt.* This is a coverage ratio which measures the number of times that this year's current maturities of long-term debt could have been repaid from cash generated by this years' operating activities.

c. **Cash used by investing activities to long-term assets:** *cash used by investing activities ÷ average long-term assets.* This ratio measures the rate at which long-term assets are being replaced. A high ratio indicates that the firm is not merely replacing assets but is growing. A low rate may indicate that the company is failing to replace long-term assets on a timely basis and faces a risk of obsolescence.

5. Compute each of the ratios below for the most recent year for your firm.

a. Cash-based return on assets = net cash flow from operating activities / average total assets

Cash-based return on assets = -- = ________

b. Cash flows to current maturities of long-term debt = net cash flow from operating activities / current maturities of long-term debt

Cash flows to current maturities of long-term debt = -------------------------------- = ________

c. Cash used by investing activities to long-term debt = cash used by investing activities / average long-term assets

Cash used by investing activities to long-term debt = ---------------------------------- = ________

6. To give perspective to the ratios computed above, check with five classmates to compare the value of the ratios for their firms to yours. Record the information bclow.

Ratio	Your Firm	CLASSMATES' FIRMS Firm 1	Firm 2	Firm 3	Firm 4	Firm 5
a. Cash-based return on assets	______	______	______	______	______	______
b. Cash flows to current maturities of long-term debt	______	______	______	______	______	______
c. Cash used by investing activities to long-term debt	______	______	______	______	______	______

7. How do your firm's cash-based ratios compare to those of your classmates' firms? Do some appear high? Some low? All about the same? Be specific. Is there anything about your firm, its industry, or your classmates' companies or industries that would tend to explain the differences between your company's ratios and those of other firms? Discuss.

8. Did your firm report any significant noncash financing and investing activities (often called direct exchanges) for its most recent year? (These usually are found at the bottom of the statement of cash flows or in a separate schedule that accompanies the statement of cash flows.)

   a. If yes, describe these transactions below. If no, write "none" below.

   b. For each item listed in (a.) above, explain how the transaction affected your firm's balance sheet.

Reading 14

Paying for Growth

TO BE IN CONTROL of your business, you have to know how much cash you need for every additional dollar in sales.

By NORM BRODSKY

There's a hard lesson we all have to learn when we go into business. The lesson is that you live or die on cash flow. Sales are nice. Profits are even nicer. But it's cash flow that determines whether or not you survive.

Where most first-time entrepreneurs trip up is in failing to understand that more sales almost always mean less cash flow — and less cash flow means trouble.

Believe me, I speak from experience here. I had no concept of the relationship between sales and cash flow when I started my first company. I thought sales were everything. If someone came and offered me a million dollars' worth of new business, my only question was, "When does it start?" I took all the business I could get, as fast as I could get it, and the company grew like crazy. Our sales went from zero to $12.8 million in five years — fast enough to put us on the 1984 Inc. 500 list. We had cash-flow problems all the way, but I didn't focus on them. I was too busy selling.

The whack on the head finally came in the form of a cash crunch that forced me to go without a salary for four straight weeks. My wife was pretty upset. "What do you mean, you can't pay yourself" she said. "I thought business was fabulous. I thought sales were going through the roof. How can business be so great, and yet you can't bring home any money for four weeks? Explain that to me. It doesn't make sense."

The truth is, I couldn't explain it to her because I didn't understand it myself — but I realized I had better figure it out. Eventually, I did.

What I learned is that you have to look ahead. You have to figure out how you're going to get the cash required to increase your sales at whatever rate you have in mind. If you don't, you run the risk of selling yourself into a corner. I'm talking about losing control of your situation, about decisions being taken away from you, about being forced to do extreme and unwise things just to stay alive.

Going without pay is the least of it. Many people stop paying their withholding taxes, which is not only illegal but stupid. Between interest and penalties, there is no more expensive money in the world. Meanwhile, your creditors are banging on your head because you can't pay your bills in an orderly fashion. It's a nightmare.

So how do you plan for growth? More precisely, how do you determine the amount of additional cash needed to cover new sales? To begin with, you have to ask the right questions about the new business coming in:

1. How much is it and over what time frame?
2. What's the gross margin?
3. How much overhead will you have to add?
4. How long will you have to wait to get paid?

If you know the answers to those four questions, you can make a rough estimate of how much extra cash you'll need.

I'll give you an example. Let's suppose you're anticipating that sales will increase by $100,000 over the next year. You have a gross margin of 30%, and you don't expect it to change because of the new business, but you know you'll have to add $10,000 in overhead for commissions, bookkeeping, whatever. You further expect your average turnover of accounts receivable (collection time) to hold steady at, say, 60 days.

Here's what you do:

Start by figuring out, cost of goods sold (COGS) on the new business — the amount of money you'll have to lay out to produce or acquire whatever you're selling. Since your gross margin is 30% of sales, your COGS is 70%, or $70,000. Add to that the extra overhead you're going to need — $10,000 — and you get $80,000 in new spending to fill $100,000 in new orders. Divide the total by the number of days in the period covered in this case, 365 and you find out that the new business is costing you $219.18 a day If you then multiply that number by the number of days it takes you to collect your receivables, you get an idea of your additional cash needs. For safety's sake, I always increase the collection period by 20%, so in this example, I'd multiply by 72 days instead of 60. The result: 72 days x $219.18 a day = $15,781. (You can try out the formula by visiting the "Paying for Growth" work sheet in *Inc. Online's* Virtual Consultant, *http://www.inc.com/virtualconsult/worksheets* on the Web.)

Understand, this is a rough, down-and-dirty formula. Some people might say it makes a number of dubious assumptions — for instance, that you pay all your own bills at once. But forecasting is inexact by definition. You need some simple tools to guide you. This one allows you to make a reasonable guess about your future cash needs, and it errs on the side of caution, which is always a good idea.

What do you do with the information? You obviously aren't going to turn away good, high margin business. So you look for ways to generate the additional cash. Maybe you can reduce the collection days on your current accounts. Maybe you can extend your accounts payable by a week or two. Maybe you make a deal with the new customers to get paid more quickly than usual.

Or maybe you go to your major vendors and say, "Listen, I have great news for both of us. I just landed a new account that's going to bring in a lot more business, but I'll have to pay you in 60 days rather than 40. Can you handle that" There are very few vendors who would say no.

Of course, as a last resort, you can always borrow the money, if you don't mind increasing your bank debt and adding to your costs. Then again, you may decide it's better to go without salary for a few weeks.

I myself haven't had to take that route in recent years and would prefer to avoid it in the future. I'm sure my wife feels the same way. She likes it when I get paid every week. So do I, for that matter. It gives us both a sense of being in control.

In business, you can't be in control if you aren't on top of your cash flow. That's a lesson worth learning as early as possible.

Inc. Magazine
October 1996
Page 29-30

QUESTIONS FOR CONSIDERATION:

1. A friend says, "A successful company is one in which sales are growing rapidly." Explain how rapidly growing sales can be a case of "too much of a good thing."

2. If you have access to the Internet, visit the web site noted in the article (http://www.inc.com) and identify other useful information that is available there.

Name: ______________________ Professor: ______________________

Course: ______________________ Section: ______________________

Assignment 15
CAPSTONE PROJECT

The purpose of this assignment is to integrate the information you have obtained about your company (or companies) and industry into a coordinated report. The report is to be typed (or word processed) and have a professional appearance. You should assume that your first post-college employer has asked you to research the firm you've been working on during this course. He/she may be considering your firm as a potential supplier, customer, competitor, or acquisition candidate. Your employer may even be secretly entertaining an offer of employment from this firm. Under any of these circumstances, you will want to present your employer with a carefully-researched, thoughtfully-written, and professionally-presented document.

COMPLETING THE ASSIGNMENT:

In general, unless modified by your professor, you have great flexibility in completing this assignment. For example, you may choose any organization structure for this report that you believe best captures and presents the necessary information. You should be creative and complete in your analyses and presentation. Generally, your report is to be based on the assignments you have completed as part of *The Financial Reporting Project*. In some cases, however, you will want to include additional information or additional creative analysis that is especially important to understanding the financial health and status of your firm (or firms) and industry. Where appropriatc, you should prepare charts or graphs to illustrate the facts you present.

Keep in mind that your employer may put your report to a variety of uses. For example, if your assigned firm is a prospective supplier, your employer would want to assess its long-run stability and its continuing ability to supply quality goods at reasonable prices. If your assigned firm is a potential customer, your employer will be concerned with its ability to meet its short-term obligations as they become due. If your assigned firm is a candidate for investment, your employer will want to understand its long-term financial structure, cost structure, and profit structure. Your report should be flexible so that it can be used in any of these ways. Regardless of the format you use, **your report must include** a summary section that states your overall assessment of the financial health and status of your firm. For example, is it strong, weak, improving, or deteriorating? Would **you** make a short-term loan to this firm? Would **you** make a long-term loan to this firm? Would **you** buy stock or invest your career with this company? Discuss why or why not.

1. **Suggested Outline:** If you are unsure how to organize your report you might consider the following outline. It follows the assignment structure of *The Financial Reporting Project.* (Be sure to check with your professor to determine if he/she has specific guidelines regarding the organization of your report.)

   a. Overview of the Industry
   b. Basic Company Information
   c. The Company's Economic, Social, Legal and Political Environment
   d. Overview of the Annual Report, SEC 10-K and Proxy Statement
   e. The Company's Independent Auditor
   f. The Income Statement
   g. Current Assets and Current Liabilities
   h. Long-Term Assets and Long-Term Liabilities
   i. Stockholders' Equity
   j. Segment Information
   k. The Cash Flow Statement
   l. Summary Statement on Financial Health and Status of the Company

   If you use this suggested outline, be careful that you don't merely make lists of the information that you collected on the assignment sheets of *The Financial Reporting Project.* The outline format of the assignments is very efficient for recording the data you found for your company, but it won't be very helpful to your employer. Remember, your employer hasn't read the articles or consulted the references that you have. You are expected to provide greater background, detail, analysis and commentary than what appears in your completed assignments.

2. **Due Date(s):** To be announced by your professor.

3. **Annual Report, SEC 10K, and Proxy Statement:** If you have not already done so, provide each of these documents to your professor when you turn in your report.

> **NOTE:** If you are part of a team in which each member is researching a different firm, avoid the temptation to write a separate report for each company and staple the reports together. Instead, this report should be an **integrated** report in which the firms are compared, contrasted, and summarized in each section. Your report must focus on comparisons and contrasts among the firms and on an integrated assessment of the overall industry situation. You will be expected to provide greater background, detail, and analysis than what appears in your individual completed assignments.

Appendix
LISTING OF SYNONYMS

One of the perplexing aspects of learning accounting is that there is so much variation in terminology. Often, two or more terms mean exactly (or very nearly) the same thing. If you don't recognize a particular term, look it up here. You may have already learned the concept or principle under a similar or different name.

ACCOUNTING TERM	ALTERNATIVE ACCOUNTING TERMS
A	
Acid-Test Ratio	Quick Ratio
Accounting Equation	Basic Accounting Equation; Balance Sheet Equation
Accounting Rate of Return	Simple Rate of Return
Allowance for Bad Debts	Allowance for Doubtful Accounts; Allowance for Uncollectible Accounts
Allowance for Doubtful Accounts	see Allowance for Bad Debts
Allowance for Uncollectible Accounts	see Allowance for Bad Debts
Annuity	Ordinary Annuity
Asset	Unexpired Cost
B	
Bad Debts Expense	Uncollectible Accounts Expense
Balance Sheet	Statement of Financial Position; Statement of Financial Condition
Balance Sheet Equation	Accounting Equation; Basic Accounting Equation
Basic Accounting Equation	Accounting Equation; Balance Sheet Equation
Basket Purchase	Lump-Sum Purchase (or acquisition); Joint Purchase; Group Purchase
Bearer Bond	Coupon Bond
Book of Original Entry	Journal; General Journal
Book Value	Carrying Value
Burden	Factory Burden; Overhead; Manufacturing Overhead
Business Entity Concept	Entity Concept; Separate Entity Concept
C	
Capital Stock	generic term for either common or preferred stock
Carrying Value	Book Value
Cash Discount	either a Sales Discount or Purchase Discount, depending on the circumstances
Cash Value	Fair Value; Fair Market Value; Market Value
Cash Equivalent Value	same as Cash Value
Charge an account	Debit an Account
Closely Held Corporation	Nonpublic Corporation
Common Stock	Capital Stock; Preferred Stock
Constant-Dollar Accounting	Price-Level Accounting; GPL Accounting
Contract (Interest) Rate	Stated Rate; Coupon Rate; Nominal Rate; Face Rate
Continuity Principle	Going Concern Principle
Contributed Capital	Paid-In Capital

Contribution Approach to Pricing	Variable Approach to Pricing
Coupon Bond	Bearer Bond
Coupon (Interest) Rate	Stated Rate; Nominal Rate; Face Rate; Contract Rate
Current Cost Accounting	Current Value Accounting
Current Ratio	Working Capital Ratio
Current Value Accounting	Current Cost Accounting

D

Debenture Bond	Unsecured Bond
Differential Cost	Incremental Cost
Direct Costing	Variable Costing
Direct Labor Efficiency Variance	Labor Efficiency Variance; Labor Usage Variance; Direct Labor Usage Variance
Direct Labor Price Variance	see Direct Labor Rate Variance
Direct Labor Rate Variance	Labor Price Variance; Direct Labor Price Variance; Labor Rate Variance
Direct Labor Usage Variance	see Direct Labor Efficiency Variance
Direct Materials Quantity Variance	Direct Materials Usage Variance; Materials Quantity Variance; Materials Usage Variance
Direct Materials Usage Variance	see Direct Materials Quantity Variance

E

Earnings	Income, Profit
Earnings Statement	Income Statement; Profit and Loss Statement
Effective Interest Rate	Market Rate; Yield Rate
Entity Principle (or concept)	Separate Entity Principle (or concept); Business Entity Principle (or concept)
Expense	Expired Cost
Expense & Revenue Summary acct	Income Summary account
Expired Cost	Expense

F

Face (Interest) Rate	Stated Rate; Coupon Rate; Nominal Rate; Contract Rate
Face Value (of bonds or notes)	Par Value; Maturity Value; Principle
Factory Burden	Burden; Overhead; Manufacturing Overhead
Fair Market Value	Fair Value; Cash Value; Market Value
Fair Value	Fair Market Value; Cash Value; Market Value
Financial Leverage	Leverage; Trading On The Equity
Fixed Assets	Plant Assets; Productive Assets; Tangible Assets; Plant, Property and Equipment
Freight-In	Transportation-In
*Funds Flow Statement	Statement of Changes in Financial Position; Statement of Changes in Financial Condition

G

Going Concern Principle	Continuity Principle
General Journal	Journal; Book of Original Entry
General Price-Level Accounting	Price-Level Accounting; Constant-Dollar Accounting
General Price-Level Gain/Loss	Price-Level Gain/Loss
Gross Margin (on sales)	Gross Profit
Gross Profit (on sales)	Gross Margin
Group Purchase	Basket Purchase; Lump-Sum Purchase, Joint Purchase

H

High Yield Bond	Junk Bond, Speculative Grade Bond
Hurdle Rate	Minimum Desired Rate (of return)

I

Income	Earnings, Profit
Income Statement	Earnings Statement; Profit and Loss Statement
Income Summary account	Expense and Revenue Summary account
Incremental Cost	Differential Cost
Internal Rate of Return	Time Adjusted Rate of Return
Inventory	Merchandise Inventory

J

Joint Purchase	Basket Purchase; Lump-sum Purchase; Group Purchase
Journal	General Journal; Book of Original Entry
Junk Bond	High Yield Bond, Speculative Grade Bond

L

Labor Efficiency Variance	see Direct Labor Efficiency Variance
Labor Price Variance	see Direct Labor Rate Variance
Labor Rate Variance	see Direct Labor Rate Variance
Labor Usage Variance	see Direct Labor Efficiency Variance
Leverage	Financial Leverage; Trading On The Equity
Lump-Sum Purchase	Basket Purchase (or acquisition); Joint Purchase; Group Purchase

M

Manufacturing Overhead	Overhead, Burden; Factory Burden
Marketable Securities	Temporary Investments; Short-term Investments
Market (Interest) Rate	Effective Rate; Yield Rate
Market Value	Fair Value; Fair Market Value; Cash Value
Materials Quantity Variance	see Direct Materials Quantity Variance
Materials Usage Variance	see Direct Materials Quantity Variance
Maturity Value (of bonds)	Face Value; Principle; Par Value
Merchandise Inventory	Inventory
Minimum Desired Rate (of return)	Hurdle Rate
Monetary Unit Principle	Unit-of-Measure Principle
Mortgage Bond	Secured Bond

N

Net Earnings	Net Income; Net Profit
Net Income	Net Profit; Net Earnings
Net Profit	Net Income; Net Earnings
Nominal Account	Temporary Account
Nominal (Interest) Rate	Stated Rate; Coupon Rate; Face Rate; Contract Rate
Nonpublic Corporation	Closely Held Corporation
Normal Operating Cycle	Operating Cycle

O

Operating Cycle	Normal Operating Cycle
Ordinary Annuity	Annuity
Ordinary Bonds	Term Bonds
Overhead	Manufacturing Overhead; Burden; Factory Burden

P

Paid-In Capital	Contributed Capital
Partnership Agreement	Partnership Contract; Articles of Co-Partnership
Par Value (of bonds)	Face Value; Principle; Maturity Value
Periodicity Principle	Time-Period Principle
Permanent Account	Real Account
Plant Assets	Fixed Assets; Plant, Property and Equipment; Productive Assets; Tangible Assets
Plant, Property and Equipment	Plant Assets; Fixed Assets; Productive Assets Tangible Assets
Preferred Stock	Capital Stock
Price-Level Accounting	Constant-Dollar Accounting; General Price-Level Accounting
Price-Level Gain/Loss	General Price-Level Gain/Loss
Principle (of bonds)	Face Value; Maturity Value; Par Value
Productive Assets	Plant Assets; Plant, Property and Equipment; Fixed Assets; Tangible Assets
Profit	Income, Earnings
Profit and Loss Statement	Income Statement; Earnings Statement
Purchase Discount	Cash Discount

Q

Quick Ratio	Acid-Test Ratio

S

Sales Discount	Cash Discount
Secured Bond	Mortgage Bond
Separate Entity Principle	Entity Principle (or concept); Business Entity Principle
Shareholders' Equity	Stockholders' Equity
Short-term Investments	Temporary Investments; Marketable Securities
Simple Rate of Return	Accounting Rate of Return
Speculative Grade Bond	Junk Bond, High Yield Bond
Stated (Interest) Rate	Coupon Rate; Face Rate; Nominal Rate; Contract Rate
*Statement of Changes in Financial Position	Funds Flow Statement; Statement of Changes in Financial Condition
*Statement of Changes in Financial Condition	Statement of Changes in Financial Position; Funds Flow Statement
Statement of Financial Position	Balance Sheet; Statement of Financial Condition
Statement of Financial Condition	Balance Sheet; Statement of Financial Position
Stockholders' Equity	Shareholders' Equity

T

Tax Avoidance	Tax Planning
Tax Planning	Tax Avoidance
Temporary Account	Nominal Account
Temporary Investments	Short-term Investments; Marketable Securities

Term Bonds	Ordinary Bonds
Time Adjusted Rate of Return	Internal Rate of Return
Time-Period Principle	Periodicity Principle
Trading On The Equity	Leverage; Financial Leverage
Transportation-In	Freight-In

U

Uncollectible Accounts Expense	Bad Debts Expense
Unexpired Cost	Asset
Unit-of-Measure Principle	Monetary Unit Principle
Unsecured Bond	Debenture Bond

V

Variable Approach to Pricing	Contribution Approach to Pricing
Variable Costing	Direct Costing

W

Working Capital Ratio	Current Ratio

Y

Yield (Interest) Rate	Market Rate; Effective Rate

*An obsolete financial statement that is no longer part of required external financial reporting. In 1987, the Financial Accounting Standards Board (FASB) decided that this statement should be deleted and replaced by the Statement of Cash Flows.